SMITHSONIAN INSTITUTION – BUREAU OF ETHNOLOGY

MYTHS

OF

THE IROQUOIS

BY

ERMINNIE A. SMITH.

with

Fourteen New, Original Drawings
by
Mohawk Artist
John Kahionhes Fadden

Reprint Series Editor - Wm. Guy Spittal

THE STORY TELLER'S BAG

Story telling is serious business. It should not be undertaken thoughtlessly, for if stories should be retold during the growing season life might come to a halt as the friendly spirits of nature become entralled by their magic spell and neglect their appointed function of providing our sustenance for the coming winter. So then also that part of the spirit which remains and wanders aimlessly when people die might be enticed into the community when stories are told, making them long again for the fellowship of the living and perhaps stealing the spirit of some new-born to keep them company. People must prepare for stories, and youngsters be protected by a buckskin thong on the wrist to tie them to this world so they might not be 'spirited' away by the dead. Just as many ceremonies must be postponed until the cold-time, so also stories should be reserved until then.

The Story Teller is an important man: a teacher and an entertainer. If he is good he will be an actor, a singer, and an enchanter who conjures from his prodigious memory. He tells the people of their real and mythic heroes from times recent and ancient; of proper behaviour and values and the consequences of evil; of why things are as they are. He tells of Who and How and Why. He deals in things gay and playful and things that are dark and mysterious and magic . . . and maybe a little dangerous.

In times past some Iroquois story tellers carried a special bag containing a variety of objects such as a miniature canoe or a skull-cracker, a tiny corn cob, a bone and more. To each of these was tied a story in the teller's mind. This is the way it was with the young boy who was the first Iroquois to be taught story telling by a talking cliff long, long ago and so it was the custom which descended from him. When an eager audience had gathered about the nightfire with the little children tumbling about, and the adults quietly waiting, he would lean forward and offer the open mouth of the bag for someone to dip into. "Hou, hasagon" . . . 'come on, take it'. Whatever was withdrawn would suggest the story he would tell. For each story a token gift from the listeners was decreed by the talking cliff of ancient times: a little tobacco, a bead, anything to show appreciation; it need not be a gift of consequence, only of gratitude. Some stories are short and can be told before a green corn husk will burn to ash; others are very long indeed and a big fire of hickory will be only coals before they have been told. If the people are responsive and his pipe is kept filled, and with maybe some of the cooling strawberry drink from time to time to keep the throat from becoming dry and scratchy like old bark, then the Story Teller might continue through the night until the new sun tells him he should stop and give thanks to Our Creator for seeing another day.

The drawing illustrates a group of Six Nations people in the clothing of the Revolutionary Period in His Majesty's American Colonies.

W.G.S.

4

CONTENTS

ILLUSTRATIONS

The four original illustrations which accompanied the 1883 edition have been replaced by the following art commissioned of Kahionhes, Mohawk artist:

MYTHS OF THE IROQUOIS.

By Erminnie A. Smith.

CHAPTER I.

GODS AND OTHER SUPERNATURAL BEINGS.

The principal monuments of the once powerful Iroquois are their myths and folk-lore, with the language in which they are embodied. As these monuments are fast crumbling away, through their contact with European civilization, the ethnologist must hasten his search among them in order to trace the history of their laws of mind and the records of their customs, ideas, laws, and beliefs. Most of these have been long forgotten by the people, who continue to repeat traditions as they have been handed down through their fathers and fathers' fathers, from generation to generation, for many centuries.

The pagan Iroquois of to-day (and there are still many) will tell you that his ancestors worshiped, as he continues to do, the "Great Spirit," and, like himself, held feasts and dances in his honor; but a careful study of the mythology of these tribes proves very clearly that in the place of one prevailing great spirit (the Indian's earliest conception of the white man's God) the Iroquois gods were numerous. All the mysterious in nature, all that which inspired them with reverence, awe, terror, or gratitude, became deities, or beings like themselves endowed with supernatural attributes, beings whose vengeance must be propitiated, mercy implored, or goodness recompensed by thank-offerings. The latter were in the form of feasts, dances, or incense.

Among the most ancient of these deities, and regarding which the traditions are the most obscure, were their most remote ancestors—certain animals who later were transformed into human shape, the names of the animals being preserved by their descendants, who have used them to designate their gentes or clans.

Many races in that particular stage of savagery when the human intellect is still in its child-like state, being impressed by the awful and incomprehensible power of Thunder, have classed it foremost among their deities, with attributes proportioned to the disposition or status of the worshiper.

Hi-nu^n, the beneficent Thunder God of the Iroquois, compares most favorably with the same god as worshiped by other races. Ever accompanied by his equally powerful assistants, his mission was understood to be only to promote the welfare of that favored people, though isolated personal offenses might demand from him a just retribution. It was therefore safe to make unto him, on his near approach to earth, his most acceptable offering, the burning tobacco, and so firmly rooted has become that ancient custom, that the aged superstitious Iroquois of to-day can often be seen making this little offering on the near approach of every thunder-storm. It is not difficult to follow the crude reasoning by which was ascribed to Hi-nu^n the goodness and glory of having destroyed the giant monsters which either poisoned the waters or infested the land. That such had existed was evident from the bones often discovered, and what power other than the crashing bolt of Hi-nu^n could have accomplished their destruction? The similarity discoverable in the myths of many peoples regarding the Thunder God and his mission of destruction to giant animals, making this an almost universal myth, is probably traceable to this simple and natural explanation, and presents no argument that the myth itself has traveled. It may, then, be safely assumed that Hi-nu^n was an indigenous god of the Iroquois, the product of their own crude reasoning powers.

Brother of the great Hi-nu^n was the West Wind, who, with him, brought from the clouds the vivifying rain, and who finally assisted the Iroquois in the extermination of the powerful stone giants. Therefore, the West Wind ranks as a beneficent deity or spirit.

The North Wind brought only calamity in its train, often killing the unripe corn and freezing the rivers, thus depriving the people of their needed sustenance, and from the mere touch of his icy fingers the benighted hunter became stiff in death. This ranked as an evil deity ever to be feared and propitiated.

Echo, the Mars of the Iroquois, only exercised his power during their wars with other tribes, in which, by repeating among the hills their cries of Go-weh, he insured their almost certain victory. He was ever honored with special thanksgiving.

Of Tă-rhu^n-hyiă-wăh-ku^n (who bore the important office of Holder of the Heavens) there is little more known than that he brought out from their mother earth the six tribes composing the Iroquois.

These are some of the Iroquois gods, a knowledge of whose existence is contained only in myths, for they belong to the charmed "mythologic age." As, however, the Iroquois tribes have not entirely passed the boundaries of that age, it is proper to mention some of their more modern divinities, in whose worship are intermingled many of their ancient ceremonies.

The "Great Spirit," so popularly and poetically known as the god of the red man, and the "Happy Hunting-ground," generally reported to be the Indian's idea of a future state, are both of them but their ready conception of the white man's God and Heaven. This is evident from a careful study of their past as gleaned from the numerous myths of their prehistoric existence.

It may be true that many of the first missionaries found them in possession of such ideas, but the Indians had long been in contact with white men from whom those ideas were obtained, and there was no incongruity in simply adding them to their former beliefs, as no fundamental change was required. They accepted the Great Spirit, but retained in many instances their former gods as his attributes, considering the thunder as his voice and the winds as his breath, and at the same time they introduced into their pagan worship a form of the trinity which is still preserved, consisting of the Great Spirit, the Sun, and Mother Earth.

Good and evil spirits also play an important rôle in Iroquoian mythology. Among the good spirits are the three sisters who still continue to preside over the favorite vegetables—corn, beans, and squashes. They are represented as loving each other very dearly and dwelling together in peace and unity. The vines of the vegetables grow upon the same soil and cling lovingly around each other. The spirit of corn is supposed to be draped with its long leaves and silken tassels. The sister who guards the bean has a wreath of its velvety pods with garments of the delicate tendrils, while the spirit of squashes is clothed with the brilliant blossoms under her care. In bright nights the sisters can be seen flitting about or heard rustling among the tall corn. To this day yearly festivals are held in their honor, and they are appealed to as "Our life, our supporters."

Among the supernatural beings corresponding to good and evil genii were the Great Heads, with ever watchful eyes, and long hair which served them as wings to bear them on missions of mercy or of destruction. This pure product of the Indian imagination figures largely in the unwritten literature of the Iroquois. There were also in those days stone giants, always the mortal enemy of man, but whose final extermination furnished the theme for wonderful stories of daring deeds performed oftentimes under the influence of charms or magic, but never in too marvelous a manner to disturb the credulity of the eager listener.

Although Atotarho and Hiawatha were contemporary personages, whose names are still continued in the list of chiefs of the present day, the myths which have accumulated around their history are so many and varied that it is impossible to define the vague boundary line separating fact from fiction. They may, therefore, be properly classed as demigods. The name of the former, which signifies "the entangled," together with his skill, cunning, and cruelty in war, soon resulted in his becoming invested with the title of a wizard. The origin of his name is attributed to his marvelous hair, which consisted of living snakes, and thus he is represented by the pictographers of his time. He is still regarded by his tribe as having been a being with supernatural endowments.

Among the same tribe, the Onondagas, are found what may be termed the "Hiawatha legends." So numerous and yet different are these stories, that they may be regarded as the histories of a long line of Hiawathas, the Hiawatha being the official name of one of the most important functionaries in the tribal government. These stories, in their relation through many generations, have at last become applied to one person, who is thus most marvelously endowed, as far surpassing all in goodness as did Atotarho in the opposite attributes. To him is ascribed the honor of having established the Great Confederacy of the Iroquois which so long rendered them invincible in war. His name, which signifies "He who seeks the wampum belt,"* probably led to the superstition of his having invented wampum. To accomplish his wonderful feats, he was provided with a magic canoe which obeyed his bidding. The legendary apotheosis accorded him, in which he is represented as ascending to Heaven in a white canoe, appears to be of modern origin.

HI-NUⁿ DESTROYING THE GIANT ANIMALS.

A hunter in the woods was once caught in a thunder-shower, when he heard a voice calling upon him to follow. This he did until he found himself in the clouds, the height of many trees from the ground. Beings which seemed to be men surrounded him, with one among them who seemed to be their chief. He was told to look below and tell whether he could see a huge water-serpent. Replying that he could not, the old man anointed his eyes, after which he could see the monster in the depths below him. They then ordered one of their number to try and kill this enemy to the human race. Upon his failing, the hunter was told to accomplish the feat. He accordingly drew his bow and killed the foe. He was then conducted back to the place where he had sought shelter from the storm, which had now ceased.

This was man's first acquaintance with the Thunder God and his assistants, and by it he learned that they were friendly toward the human race, and protected it from dragons, serpents, and other enemies.

A SENECA LEGEND OF HI-NUⁿ AND NIAGARA.

A beautiful Indian maiden was about to be compelled by her family to marry a hideous old Indian.

* This is the interpretation given by the tribe, the real meaning, as Pére Cuoq suggests, being a "river maker," which implies alliance between nations, and as wampum was used for treaties, the original idea seems to have been retained after the word itself has become denotive.

Despair was in her heart. She knew that there was no escape for her, so in desperation she leaped into her canoe and pushed it from shore on the roaring waters of Niagara. She heeded not that she was going to her death, preferring the angry waters to the arms of her detested lover.

Now, the God of Cloud and Rain, the great deity Hi-nu^n, who watches over the harvest, dwelt in a cave behind the rushing waters. From his home he saw the desperate launching of the maiden's canoe ; saw her going to almost certain destruction. He spread out his wings and flew to her rescue, and caught her just as her frail bark was dashing on the rocks below.

The grateful Indian girl lived for many weeks in Hi-nu^n's cave. He taught her many new things. She learned from him why her people died so often—why sickness was always busy among them. He told her how a snake lay coiled up under the ground beneath the village, and how he crept out and poisoned the springs, because he lived upon human beings and craved their flesh more and more, so that he could never get enough if they died from natural causes.

Hi-nu^n kept the maiden in till he learned that the ugly old suitor was dead. Then he bade her return and tell her tribe what she had learned of the great Hi-nu^n.

She taught them all he had told her and begged them to break up their settlement and travel nearer to the lake; and her words prevailed. For a while sickness ceased, but it broke out again, for the serpent was far too cunning to be so easily outwitted. He dragged himself slowly but surely after the people, and but for Hi-nu^n's influence would have undermined the new settlement as he had the former one. Hi-nu^n watched him until he neared the creek, then he launched a thunderbolt at him. A terrible noise awoke all the dwellers by the lake, but the snake was only injured, not killed. Hi-nu^n was forced to launch another thunderbolt, and another and another, before, finally, the poisoner was slain.

The great dead snake was so enormous that when the Indians laid his body out in death it stretched over more than twenty arrow flights, and as he floated down the waters of Niagara it was as if a mountain appeared above them. His corpse was too large to pass the rocks, so it became wedged in between them and the waters rose over it mountains high. As the weight of the monster pressed on the rocks they gave way and thus the horseshoe form, that remains to this day, was fashioned. But the Indians had no more fever in their settlement.

THE THUNDERERS.

The following story, as related to me by Horatio Hale, who received it from an Indian chief, shows that sustained imaginative power which seems to distinguish the myths of the Iroquoian family.

On one occasion in the ancient time three warriors set out on an expedition. When they were far distant from their own land, one of them had the misfortune to break his leg. By the Indian law it became the duty of the others to convey their injured comrade back to his home. They formed a rude litter, and, laying him upon it, bore him for some distance.

At length they came to a ridge of mountains. The way was hard and the exertion severe. To rest themselves, they placed their burden on the ground. They withdrew to a little distance and took evil counsel together. There was a deep hole, or pit, opening into the ridge of the mountain at a little distance from the place where they were sitting. Returning to the litter, they took up their helpless load, carried him near the brink of the pit, and suddenly hurled him in. Then they set off rapidly for their own country. When they arrived they reported that he had died of wounds received in fight. Great was the grief of his mother, a widow, whose only support he had been. To soothe her feelings they told her that her son had not fallen into the enemy's hands. They had rescued him, they said, from that fate, had carefully tended him in his last hours, and had given his remains a becoming burial.

They little imagined that he was still alive. When he was thrown down by his treacherous comrades he lay for some time insensible at the bottom of the pit. When he recovered his senses, he observed an old gray-headed man seated near him, crouching into a cavity on one side of the pit. "Ah, my son," said the old man, "what have your friends done to you?" "They have thrown me here to die, I suppose," he replied, with true Indian stoicism. "You shall not die," said the old man, "if you will promise to do what I require of you in return for saving you." "What is that?" asked the youth. "Only that when you recover you will remain here and hunt for me and bring me the game you kill." The young warrior readily promised, and the old man applied herbs to his wound and attended him skillfully until he recovered. This happened in the autumn. All through the winter the youth hunted in the service of the old man, who told him that whenever he killed any game too large for one man to carry, he would come himself and help to convey it to the pit, in which they continued to reside. When the spring arrived, bringing melting snows and frequent showers, he continued his pursuit of the game, though with more difficulty. One day he encountered an enormous bear, which he was lucky enough to kill. As he stooped to feel its fatness and judge of its weight, he heard a murmur of voices behind him. He had not imagined that any human beings would find their way to that lonely region at that time of the year. Astonished, he turned and saw three men, or figures in the shape of men, clad in strange cloud-like garments, standing near him. "Who are you?" he asked. In reply they informed him that they were the Thunderers (Hi-nu^{n}). They told him that their mission was to keep the earth and everything upon it in good order for the benefit of the human race. If there was a drought, it was their duty to bring rain; if there were serpents or other noxious creatures, they were commissioned to destroy them, and, in short, to do away with everything injurious to mankind. They told him that their present object was to destroy the old man to whom he had bound himself, and who, as they would show him, was a very different sort of being from what he pretended to be. For this they required his aid. If he would assist them he would do a good act, and they would convey him back to his home, where he would see his mother and be able to take care of her. This proposal and their assurances overcame any reluctance the young man might have felt to sacrifice his seeming benefactor. He went to him and told him that he had killed a bear and needed his help to bring it home. The old man was anxious and uneasy: He bade the youth examine the sky carefully and see if there was the smallest speck of cloud visible. The young man replied that the sky was perfectly clear. The old man then came out of the hollow and followed the young hunter, urging him constantly to make haste, and looking upward with great anxiety. When they reached the bear they cut it up hurriedly with their knives, and the old man directed the youth to place it all on his shoulders. The youth complied, though much astonished at his companion's strength. The old man set off hastily for the pit, but just then a cloud appeared and the thunder rumbled in the distance. The old man threw down his load and started to run. The thunder rumbled nearer, and the old man assumed his proper form of an enormous porcupine, which fled through the bushes, discharging its quills like arrows backward as it ran. But the thunder followed him, with burst upon burst, and finally a bolt struck the huge animal, which fell lifeless into its den.

Then the Thunderers said to the young man, "Now, that we have done our work here, we will take you to your home and your mother, who is grieving for you all the time."

They gave him a dress like that which they wore, a cloud-like robe, having wings on its shoulders, and told him how these were to be moved. Then he rose with them in the air, and soon found himself in his mother's cornfield. It was night. He went to her cabin, and drew aside the mat which covered the opening. The widow started up and gazed at him in the moonlight with terror, thinking that she saw her son's ghost. He guessed her thoughts. "Do not be alarmed, mother," he said; "it is no ghost. It is your son come back to take care of you." As may be supposed, the poor woman was overjoyed, and welcomed her long-lost son with delight. He remained with her, fulfilling his duties as a son, for the rest of the year. What was done to his treacherous comrades is not recorded. They were too insignificant to be further noticed in the story, which now assumes a more decided mythological character.

When the Thunderers bade farewell to the young man they said to him, "We will leave the cloud-dress with you. Every spring, when we return, you can put it on and fly with us to be witness to what we do for the good of man." Accordingly, the youth hid the dress in the woods, that no one might see it, and waited until the spring. Then the Thunderers returned, and he resumed the robe, and floated with them in the clouds over the earth. As they passed above a mountain he became thirsty, and seeing below him a pool he descended to drink of it. When he rejoined his companions they looked at him, and saw that the water with which his lips were moist had caused them to shine as if smeared with oil. "Where have you been drinking?" they asked him eagerly. "In yonder pool," he answered, pointing to where it lay still in sight. They said, "There is something in that pool which we must destroy. We have sought it for years, and now you have happily found it for us." Then they cast a mighty thunderbolt into the pool, which presently became dry. At the bottom of it, blasted by the thunder, was an immense grub, of the kind which destroys the corn and beans and other products of the fields and gardens; but this was a vast creature ("as big as a house," said the chief), the special patron and representative of all grubs. After accompanying his spirit friends to some distance, and seeing more of their good deeds of the like sort, the youth returned home and told his friends that the Thunder was their divine protector, and narrated the proofs which he had witnessed of this benignant character. Thence originated the honor in which the Thunder is held among the Indians. Many Iroquois still call Hi-nu^{n} their grandfather.

ECHO GOD.

When engaged in wars with different nations the voice of the Echo God served for signals, as it would only respond to the calls of Iroquois. At the coming of evening it was used by them to call in those who were out on the war-path. When the warrior would whoop the Echo God would take it up and carry it on through the air, the enemy not being able to hear it, as this was the special god of the Six Nations. Therefore when they had gained a great victory a dance was held to give praise to this god. When enemies were killed their victors called out as many times as there were persons killed, the cry being "Goh-weh! Goh-weh!" "I'm telling you!" These words the Echo God took up and repeated. But if one of their own tribe was killed they called out, "Oh-weh! Oh-weh!" meaning "Our own!"

After any of these signals were given all assembled together to hold council and make arrangements for an attack or pursuit. Then were sent out runners, who also proclaimed. If no response was made by the Echo God it was an omen that they should not start, but they continued calling, and if the god still remained silent, a service was held to ask the cause of his anger.

When a warfare was ended victoriously a dance was held to the Echo God and the nations assembled to rejoice—but first to mourn for the dead and decide on the fate of the captives. As the Echo God was never called upon except in emergencies during warfare, now since wars are over the feast and dance to the Echo God have ceased to be a part of the Iroquois ceremonies.

EXTERMINATION OF THE STONE GIANTS.

Related by Mr. O'BEILLE BEILLE, grandson of Cornplanter.

The stone giants, who principally inhabited the far West, resolved to come East and exterminate the Indians. A party of Senecas, just starting out on the war-path, were warned of their impending danger and were bidden to accept the challenge to fight the stone giants and appoint a time and place. This they did. At the appointed time the giants appeared at the place, which was near a great gulf. Then there came a mighty wind from the west which precipitated the whole race of giants down into the abyss, from which they were never able to extricate themselves, and the God of the West Wind was ever after held in reverence by the Senecas.

THE NORTH WIND.

It was the custom at a certain season for the medicine men to go about demanding gifts of the people; but an icy figure had also appeared, demanding a man as a sacrifice; whereupon the Thunder God was appealed to, and he came to the rescue with his assistants and chased the figure far into the north, where they doomed the icy demon to remain. To this day his howling and blustering are heard, and when any venturesome mortal dares to intrude too far towards his abode his frosty children soon punish the offender. He is termed Kă-tăsh-hŭaht, or North Wind, and ranks as an evil spirit.

GREAT HEAD.

It was a common belief among Indians that there was a strange, human-like creature, consisting simply of a head made terrific with large eyes and covered with long hair. His home was upon a huge rock, a rifted promontory, over which his long hair streamed in shaggy fierceness.

Seen or unseen, if he saw anything that had the breath of life he growled: "Kûⁿñ″-kuⁿ, Kuⁿñ″-kuⁱⁿ, wă″-h-tci′-ha″-i-h"; that is, "I see thee, I see thee, thou shalt die," or "thou shalt suffer."

In a distant wilderness there lived a man and his wife with ten children, all boys. In the course of events the father died, and was soon followed by the mother of the boys, who were now left alone with their uncle. They were greatly afflicted by the loss of both parents but after a while resumed their hunting for support.

As was customary, the older brothers went to their hunting grounds and the younger ones staid at home. One day they looked for the return of their elder brother in vain; they also looked in vain for the second brother's return. Then the oldest of those at home said, "I will go to look them up"; and he went off, but did not return that night. The next brother then went to hunt for his lost brothers. He also did not return, and thus it was with all until the youngest brother was left alone with his aged uncle.

The youngest brother was forbidden to go away from home lest he too should be lost. One day the two were out in the woods, when the younger one, stepping over a log, heard a noise like a groan, which seemed to come from the earth. The groan being repeated, they concluded to dig into the earth, where they discovered a man covered with mould, and taking him and setting him up they saw some signs of life and were convinced that he was alive. Then the old man said to the lad, "Run for the bear's oil." When brought, they rubbed it over him, and at last were well pleased to see returning consciousness.

In caring for him they at first fed him on oil until he began to move his eyes and talk. The strange man then told them that he did not know how long he had been there, that all he knew was that the last time he went out was to hunt. They persuaded him to stay with them, whereupon he related the story of the nine brothers who had so mysteriously disappeared. They then discovered that the stranger was somewhat supernatural, for he told them very strange things.

One night he said, "I cannot sleep; hearken to the great noise in this direction. I know what it is—it is my brother, the Great Head, who is howling through this hurricane. He is an awful being, for he destroys those who go near him." "Is he your brother?" "Yes, own brother." "If you sent for him would he come here?" "No," he replied; "but perhaps I might entice him to come here. I will try; but if he comes you must make great provision for him; you must cut a huge maple tree into blocks, for that is what he eats." The stranger inquired how far he would be obliged to go to find the home of the "Head." The uncle replied, "You would get there about noon." Early the next morning he took his bow and started. When he came to a hickory tree he pulled it up, and from its roots he made arrows, and then ran onward until he came to a place answering the description given him, near which he was to find the end of his journey. Remembering that he was warned to look out for the "Great Eyes," which would be sure to see him, he called for a mole, to which he said, "I am going in this direction and I want you to creep down under the grass where you will not be seen." Having gone into the mole, he at last saw the Great Head through the blades of grass. Ever watchful, the head cried out "Kunñ-kun," "I see thee." The man in the mole saw that the "Head" was watching an owl, then drawing his bow, he shot an arrow into the Great Head, crying, "I came after you." The arrow as it flew to its mark became very large, but as it was returning became as small as when it left the bow. Thereupon, taking the arrow, he ran swiftly toward home; but he had not gone far when he heard a great noise like the coming of a storm. It was the Great Head riding on a tempest. Unshaken by this, he continued to run until he saw that the Great Head was coming down to the spot where he was, when he drew his bow again, and as the arrow left the bow it became larger as it sped, and it drove the Great Head away as before it had done. These maneuvers were repeated many times. In the meanwhile the uncle had prepared a mallet, and now he heard the rush and roar of the coming hurricane and said, "The stranger has allured him home." He now went to the door and said, "We must hammer him ; here, take this mallet." As the Great Head came bursting through the door, the two men industriously plied their mallets to it. At this proceeding, the Great Head began to laugh, thus: "Si-h si-h si-h," for he was pleased to see his brother. When the tumult had subsided, the uncle asked the Great Head to remain, and gave him to eat the blocks which had been prepared for him. Then the two men told the Great Head about the brothers who were lost and about the stranger. Then the Great Head said, "I know where they have gone; they have gone to a place where lives a woman who is a witch and who sings continually."

Now, the Great Head said, "I have been here long enough; I want to go home; this young man is pretty bright, and if he wishes to go to see this witch, I will show him her abode and all the bones of his brothers." The young man consenting, he and the Great Head started on the morrow, and finally came to a place where they heard this song: "Dy-giñ-nyă-de, he''-oñ-we, he'-oñ-we-ni''-ă-h gi-di-oñ-ni-ăh," which the witch was singing. At length she spoke and said "Schis-t-ki-añ"; this was the magical word at which, when heard, all turned to dry bones. Upon hearing this the Great Head said, "I will ask the question, 'How long have you been here?' and the hair will fall from my head and you must replace it, and it will grow fast, and then I will bite her flesh and pull it from her, and as it comes off you must take it from my mouth and throw it off, saying 'Be a fox, a bird, or anything else,' and it will then run off never to return."

They did as they had planned, and when the witch begged for mercy the Great Head said, "You had no mercy ; see the dry bones; you must die": and so they killed her, and her flesh was turned into animals, and birds, and fish.

When she had died, the Head said, "Let us burn her to ashes." When this was done, the Head said, "Let us search for the year-old bones and cause them to lie in rows," and they worked together selecting those they thought were bones of the nine brothers, and placed them together. When this was done, the Great Head said, "I am going to my old home in the great mountain, and when I fly over here on a tempest then you say to these bones, 'All arise,' and they all will rise and you may go home with them." Great Head departed, and then arose a storm and a terrific hurricane, and the Great Head out of the wind called to the nine brothers to awake, and they all arose to life, shouting for joy at seeing each other and their youngest brother again.

CUSICK'S STORY OF THE DISPERSION OF THE GREAT HEADS.

An old squaw who resided at Onondaga was alone in her wigwam one evening. While sitting by the fire parching some acorns one of the monstrous heads made its appearance at the door. Thinking that the woman was eating coals of fire, by which these monsters were put to flight, it suddenly disappeared, and none of its kind have been seen since that day.

THE STONE GIANT'S WIFE.

In the olden days the hunters always took their wives with them on their expeditions. It was a wife's duty to fetch home the game that was killed and prepare and cook it.

A great hunter set forth upon a hunting excursion and took his wife with him. He found so much game that finally he built a wigwam and settled down. One day he had gone hunting in one direction while his wife was sent in another to collect the game he had killed the previous day.

When she returned towards home one evening, laden with game, she was surprised at hearing a woman's voice, and as she entered her surprise changed to fear, for she saw a stone giant woman nursing the chief's child. "Do not be afraid," said the giantess; "come in." And as the wife obeyed she told her that she had run away from her cruel husband, who wanted to kill her, and that she wished to stay a while with the hunter's family. She had come from very far, from the land of the Stone Giants, and was very tired, and added that they must be careful what food they gave her. She could not eat raw food, but it must be well cooked, so thoroughly cooked, indeed, that she could not taste the blood, for if she once tasted blood she might wish to kill them and the child and eat them. She knew that the woman's husband was a mighty hunter, and she knew that his wife brought in the game, but now she would do it instead; then she said that she knew where to find it and would start after it at once.

After a while she returned, bringing in one hand a load which four ordinary men could not have carried. The woman cooked it, and they dined together.

As evening came on the Stone Giantess bade the woman go out and meet her husband and tell him of her visit; so she started, and the hunter was much pleased to hear of the help she had given.

In the morning, after he had gone on his hunting expedition, the giantess said, "Now I have a secret for you: My husband is after me. In three days he will be here. We shall have a terrible fight when he comes, and you and your husband must help me to kill him."

In two days afterwards she said, "Now your husband must remain at home, for mine is coming. But do not be afraid; we shall kill him, only you must help catch and hold him. I will show you where to strike him so that the blow will go right through to his heart." The hunter and his wife were both frightened at this, but she reassured them, and they all three awaited the coming of the giant. So she placed herself in the entrance, and as he came in sight she was ready. She seized him and threw him on the ground. "Now," she said, "strike him on the arms, now on the back of the neck"; and so he was finally killed. Then said she, "I will take him out and bury him," which she did.

She staid a while quietly with the hunter and his wife, fetching in the game and being useful until they were ready to leave and return to the settlement. Then she said, "Now I must go home to my people, for I need fear nothing." So she bade them farewell.

And this is the end of the story of the Stone Giantess.

THE STONE GIANT'S CHALLENGE.

A Stone Giant challenged a Seneca chief to a race. The challenge was accepted, and the time for the start appointed two days later.

The hunter employed the time in making a pair of moccasins, and in due time the race began. The hunter was in advance; he led the way over cornfields and through bushes, over and around brooks, and went a weary distance until he was very tired and his moccasins were nearly worn off his feet. At last he began to climb rocks. Now, the Stone Giant had no power to raise his head and could not tell where the hunter was when once he was above him, and in this dilemma he had recourse to a charm, and took from his pocket a human finger. He placed it upright upon his hand, and it immediately pointed the way for him to go.

Now, the hunter had turned and seen him do it, so he stooped and snatched the charm from him, whereupon the giant commenced crying and said: "You have won. You have taken my charm, and now you can always find game and all you want, for the finger will direct you to it."

HIAWATHA AND THE IROQUOIS WAMPUM.

In one of his missions into the country of the Mohawks, Hiawatha once came upon the borders of a lake. While deliberating in what manner he should cross it, the whole sky became filled with wild ducks, all of which finally alighted upon the surface of the water. After quenching their thirst and soaking their plumage they ascended again into the air in one great mass, and lo! the lake had become dry, while its bed was filled with shells.

From these the wise chief and counselor proceeded to make the wampum which afterward so firmly cemented the union of the six tribes, thereby forming the great Iroquois Confederacy.

CHAPTER II.

PIGMIES.

Another creation of the fertile Indian fancy consists of the race of pigmies, Lilliputian in size, but mighty in skill and deed. They carved out the beauties of rock, cliff, and cave, but also, like Hi·nuⁿ, they were endowed with the mightier power of destroying the monster animals which endangered the life of man. Cliff, rock, and grotto attested the skill of that departed race, and the exhumed bones of giant animals bore as perfect witness to the truth of their existence as did the "Homo diluviæ testis" of a century ago to the truth of the story of the deluge.

THE WARRIOR SAVED BY PIGMIES.

It was customary for the Iroquois tribes to make raids upon the Cherokees while the latter inhabited the swamps of Florida.

One of these raiding parties had been away from home about two years, and on the very evening of the journey homeward one of its number was taken quite ill. After a long consultation (the man continuing to grow worse), the party concluded to leave him, and when they had reached one of the rivers of the Alleghany Mountains they abandoned him on the shore. After their arrival at home the warriors were questioned in regard to the missing war-chief. In reply, they said that they did not exactly know what had become of him, and that he must have been lost or killed in the "Southern country."

During the night the sick chief lying on the bank heard the soft sounds of a canoe's approach, and saw three male pigmies landing hurriedly. Finding him, they bade him to lie there until they returned, as they were going to a neighboring "salt-lick" where many strange animals watered, and where they were to watch for some of them to come up out of the earth.

Reaching the place the pigmies found that the animals had not come out from the ground. They hid themselves and soon saw a male buffalo approach. The beast looked around and began to drink, and immediately two buffalo cows arose out of the lick.

The three animals, after quenching their thirst, lay down upon the bank.

The pigmies seeing that the animals were becoming restless and uneasy, concluded wisely to shoot them, and succeeded in killing the two buffalo cows.

They returned to the man and told him that they would care for him.

This they did, and brought him to his friends, who from his story learned that the returned warriors were false, and they were accordingly punished.

From a strong desire to see the "lick," a large party searched for it and found it surrounded with bones of various large animals killed by the pigmies.

THE PIGMIES AND THE GREEDY HUNTERS.

The following story is told as having actually occurred:

Mr. Johnson and others of the Seneca Reservation went out on a hunting expedition to a region quite remote from their homes. Upon their arrival at the hunting grounds they found game so plentiful that they were obliged to throw away large quantities of meat to enable them to preserve and carry the skins of the many animals they had slain.

Several months after their arrival they moved farther into the wilderness, and found, to their sorrow, that game was growing scarcer each day until they could find none. As a consequence of their prodigality they were soon in want of that very meat which they had so wantonly thrown away, and were finally pushed to the verge of starvation.

At length a pigmy appeared to the hapless hunters, and said that their present condition was a just punishment to them for their wastefulness and greed for gain. In despair the hunters inquired of the pigmy what they must do to obtain food. The pigmy said that they must either starve or give up all the skins and furs which they had collected and prepared for use. The hunters asked how long they would be permitted to consider the proposition. The pigmy replied that when they had decided they could call one of his race by simply tapping on a rock, and then they could tell their decision.

Not agreeing upon any answer after a long consultation, they called one of the pigmies to ask for better terms. The hunters said they would rather die than submit, if the amount of food were small, since, with a small supply and being in a strange, unknown country, they could not possibly find their way home. They further asked him to show them their homeward journey. The pigmy said that he could not grant their request without the full concurrence of his race, but that he would give them food enough to satisfy them in their present distress. He then showed them into a capacious and furnished cavern, in which they were to await the answer of the pigmies.

On the following day the pigmy returned and said they had been forgiven for their wastefulness, and that they would be furnished with provisions without parting with their furs. He said that the hunters must remain in the cavern, and that some time in the night they would be called for.

About midnight they were awakened and found themselves in their first camping-ground.

The Senecas were informed that they were brought there by their ever-vigilant pigmy friends.

THE PIGMY'S MISSION.

There was once a pigmy living in a little cave. Near him dwelt a hunter in a wigwam. The pigmy sent to him and bade him visit him. The hunter went accordingly, and saw many wonderful things; the little people themselves in great numbers, and the corn and huckleberries and other berries which they had in plenty to eat. And the pigmy said: "This is our home, and all we have is given to us free, and although I am small I am stronger than you." Then he showed him the games, and the bows and arrows and the dances, even the war dances and the hunter said when he had seen it all, "Let me go." But the pigmy said, "Stay! Do you know my name? I am called Go-Ga-Ah (little fellow). I had my choice of name. I will let you out when I have told you our mission. We are to help you, and we have never injured you, but now we are going to move away from here. We are going where there is more danger from the giant animals, that we may help those who need our aid." Then having finished his speech, he opened the door and let the hunter go on his way.

CHAPTER III.

PRACTICE OF SORCERY.

The early history of the races of mankind, now civilized, is marked in all its course known to us by a belief in mysterious powers and influences. Sorcerers, men believed to be skilled in occult arts, have been known among them all. An examination into the actual practice of sorcery or magical arts among savage and barbaric tribes is therefore of peculiar interest.

In none of the myths of the Iroquois which I have reason to believe antedate the appearance of Europeans do I find anything indicating a belief in Heaven or a separate spiritual world, although some of their customs indicate that they may have had such a notion. The only word for Heaven in the different dialects is evidently a literal translation of the Christian idea, and signifies " in the sky." It would seem that after the possession of that idea came the desire for intermediaries between living men and a spiritual world, indicating the first step toward a higher philosophy.

Among the highly civilized Chaldeans, Egyptians, and Greeks, the success of magic depended upon the ignorance of the masses and the comparative learning of the few who practiced it. Among the Indians the knowledge of the medicine man and the more expert sorceress is little above that of the body of the tribe. Their success depends entirely upon their own belief in being supernaturally gifted, and upon the faith and fear of their followers. I do not believe that the Iroquois lives to-day who is not a believer in sorcery or who would not in the night time quail at seeing a bright light the nature of which he did not understand. The most intelligent, the wisest, and the best Christian whom I ever met among them told me of the wonderful marvels he himself had wrought. He had stayed the flames of a burning church by holding forth his right hand. He had lamed for life a man who was stealing cherries by pointing his finger at him. Few bad Indians came into his presence without begging him not to " bewitch" them. This good Tuscarora ranks as one of the leading Christians of his tribe and lives up to all the moral precepts of the Bible, from which he can quote a text considered by himself to be appropriate for each of the superstitions in which he so firmly believes.

A few Tuscarora names with their definitions will serve to illustrate some of the practices and beliefs of the Iroquois.

Yă-ku-wi-săt: A person possessing within himself a live crystal which he could call from his mouth or nose. The crystal placed in a gourd of water, rendered visible the apparition of a person who had bewitched

another. By applying this crystal to one bewitched, hairs, straws, leaves, pebbles, &c., could be drawn forth.

Rhu^{n}ñ-ta-yä : A medicine man who by the use of a small kettle boiled roots or herbs, and by covering the head with a blanket and holding it over the kettle could see the image of an enemy who had bewitched either some one else or himself.

Yä-tyu^{n}ñ-yú^{n}ñ : One who performed miraculous feats by drawing out with alder tubes, hairs, pieces of skin, leaves, &c., from people who had been bewitched with these things.

Ră-nú^n-kwă-terha-yu^n-nä-rhi : Superior medicine man.

Us-ku^n-rhă-rhih : A carnivorous ghost bodied forth in a skeleton.

U-h nä$''$-wăk : A departing ghost who will revisit its dead body.

U-t-ku^n-terhă$''$-ks^{n}ñ : An evil spirit, from whom all witches received their power.

U-ht-kú^n-sü rhú^n : One who could assume a partly animal shape.

Yä-skú^n-nú^n-nä : The ghost of a living person.

Yä tcu^{n}ñ-hu-h-kwă-kwä : An apparition which could emit flames of light.

U-h-t-kú^n : A natural-born witch or ghost.

Nä-yú^n-h-nă-nyä-rhú^{n}ñ-nyä^n-a : A witch under the influence or power of a superior witch.

Stories abound in which these personages or spirits are introduced. The belief in *Yä-sku^{n}ñ-nu^n-nä*, or that the spirit of a person could be in one locality and its body exist at the same time in another, explains much of the phenomena of witchcraft, and accounts for the strange confessions oftentimes made by those who were known to have been unjustly accused.

Many customs still existing show that spirits are supposed to continue to experience the wants of humanity after leaving the body. For some time after the death of an adult his accustomed portion of food is often dealt out for the supposed hungry spirit, and on the death of a nursing child two pieces of cloth are saturated with the mother's milk and placed in the hands of the dead child so that its spirit may not return to haunt the bereaved mother.

When a living nursing child is taken out at night the mother takes a pinch of white ashes and rubs it on the face of the child so that the spirits will not trouble it, because they say that a child still continues to hold intercourse with the spirit world whence it so recently came.

THE ORIGIN OF WITCHES AND WITCH CHARMS.

A great many years ago boys were instructed to go out and hunt birds and other game for the support of their respective families and to learn from practice how to hunt. A certain boy while out hunting came across a beautiful snake. Taking a great fancy to it, he caught it and cared for it, feeding it on birds, &c., and made a bark bowl in which he kept it. He put fibers, down, and small feathers into the water with the snake, and soon found that these things had become living beings. From this fact he naturally conjectured that the snake was endowed with supernatural powers. He then continued his experiments, and discovered that whatever he put into this water became alive; so he went to another swamp and got other snakes, which he put into the bowl. While experimenting he saw other Indians putting things on their eyes to see sharp, so he rubbed some of this snake-water on his eyes, and climbing a tree he found that he could see things even if they were hidden.

Finding that this snake liquid was powerful enough to improve his sight, he concluded that the more snakes he put into the waters the more powerful would be the liquid. He therefore hung a large number of snakes so that their oil dropped into the water, increasing its power and making more lively its strange inhabitants.

He then learned that by simply putting one of his fingers into the liquid and pointing it at any person that person would immediately become bewitched.

After placing some roots (which were not poisonous) into the snake liquid, he put some of the mixture into his mouth and found that it produced a peculiar sensation. By blowing it from his mouth it would give a great light; by placing some in his eyes he could see in the dark and could go through all kinds of impassable places; he could become like a snake; he could even become invisible, and could travel faster than any other mortal. An arrow dipped into this liquid and shot at any living being, even if it did not hit its object, would nevertheless kill it. A feather dipped into this snake water and then pointed at any wished-for game, would immediately start for the desired thing and would always kill it, and when the game was dissected the feather was always found in it. Having discovered the great power of this snake extract, he took into consideration the finding of counteracting agents. To accomplish this end, he diligently searched for roots and herbs having the required qualities, and finally he was rewarded by obtaining antidotes which would work upon objects which he had bewitched or wounded.

ORIGIN OF THE SENECA MEDICINE

Nearly two hundred years ago a man went into the woods on a hunting expedition. He was quite alone. He camped out in a field and was wakened in the night by the sound of singing and a noise like the beating of a drum. He could not sleep any more, so he rose and went in the direction of the sound. To his surprise the place had all the appearance of being inhabited. On the one hand was a hill of corn, on the other a large squash vine with three squashes on it, and three ears of corn grew apart from all the others. He was unable to guess what it meant, but started off on his hunting once more, determined to return some evening, being both curious and uneasy. In the night, as he slept near by, he again heard a noise, and awakening, saw a man looking at him, who said, "Beware! I am after you; what you saw was sacred; you deserve to die." But the people who now gathered around said they would pardon it, and would tell him the secret they possessed: "The great medicine for wounds," said the man who had awakened him, "is squash and corn; come with me and I will teach you."

He led him to the spot where the people were assembled, and there he saw a fire and a laurel bush which looked like iron. The crowds danced around it singing, and rattling gourd-shells, and he begged them to tell him what they did it for.

Then one of them heated a stick and thrust it right through his cheek, and then applied some of the medicine to prove to him how quickly it could heal the wound. Then they did the same to his leg. All the time they sang a tune; they called it the "medicine song," and taught it to him.

Then he turned to go home, and all at once he perceived that they were not human beings, as he had thought, but animals, bears, beavers, and foxes, which all flew off as he looked. They had given him directions to take one stalk of corn and dry the cob and pound it very fine, and to take one squash, cut it up and pound that, and they then showed him how much for a dose. He was to take water from a running spring, and always from up the stream, never down.

He made up the prescription and used it with very great success, and made enough before he died to last over one hundred years.

This was the origin of the great medicine of the Senecas. The people sing over its preparation every time the deer changes his coat, and when it is administered to a patient they sing the medicine song, while they rattle a gourd-shell as accompaniment, and burn tobacco. Burning tobacco is the same as praying. In times of trouble or fear, after a bad dream, or any event which frightens them, they say, "My mother went out and burned tobacco."

The medicine is prepared now with the addition of meat.

A "TRUE" WITCH STORY.

Among the Senecas dwelt an old woman who was very stingy. All at once she began to suffer great pain in her eye. She consulted a conjurer, who went out to a bush and covered it with a tent and then began to sing, keeping time with his hand. After a while he returned to her and said: "You are bewitched. You refused to give milk to a poor woman who came to beg of you, and she has bewitched you. I have had her house revealed to me, and I saw her, but she was combing her hair over her face, so I could not see her features. I would not recognize her again."

Next day he tried again; then he said: "Now I know who she is." So they sent for a chief and told him all about it, and he brought the woman before them. She was a Chippewa and a witch. The chief had her brought to the old woman's cabin. She owned that she had bewitched her, and said, "Fetch me the thigh-bone of a beaver from a man who is the child of Molly Brant, the child of Governor W. Johnson." The bone was brought, and by the time it arrived she had scoured a brass kettle, and had clean water poured into it. As soon as she received the bone, which was hollow, she placed it against the eye that was not painful and spat through it. After a while she ceased spitting, and looked in the water. A spider was running around in the kettle. She covered it over with her handkerchief, then removed it, and a feather lay there instead of the spider. The pain left the old woman but the sight was not restored.

A CASE OF WITCHCRAFT.

The victim in this case was a Mary Jemison, who, having severe pains in her chest, concluded that she was bewitched, and consulted the witch-doctors, who applied their extractive bandages, which greatly relieved her. She saw a dog as an apparition coming toward her, and directed her friends to shoot it, but they did not succeed in killing it. In like manner a cat, which was invisible to other people, was seen by her. She finally recovered, but Andrew John, who was pronounced her bewitcher, and who was outwitched, is now dying from consumption.

AN INCANTATION TO BRING RAIN.

In a dry season, the horizon being filled with distant thunder-heads, it was customary to burn what is called by the Indians real tobacco as an offering to bring rain.

On occasions of this nature the people were notified by swift-footed heralds that the children, or sons, of Thunder were in the horizon, and that tobacco must be burned in order to get some rain. Every family was supposed to have a private altar upon which its offerings were secretly made; after which said family must repair, bearing its tithe,

to the council-house, where the gathered tithes of tobacco were burned in the council-fire. While the tobacco was burning, the agile and athletic danced the rain-dance.

When this was done, Hi-nû^n, pleased with the incense of the burning tobacco, called forth huge dark banks of rain clouds and took personal charge of the gathering storm to guide it to wet the dry and parched earth. Hi-nû^n was considered a great lover of tobacco, but always in want of it.

A CURE FOR ALL BODILY INJURIES.

This was made from the dried and pulverized flesh of every known bird, beast, and fish. Equal portions of this flesh were mixed into a compound, which was divided among all true medicine-men.

A WITCH IN THE SHAPE OF A DOG.

Witches could and did assume animal shapes.

On the Buffalo Reservation a man saw a "witch-woman" coming, with fire streaming from her mouth. Crossing a creek and obtaining his gun the man returned and saw a dog at no great distance resting its forefeet upon a log, and it had fire streaming from its mouth and nostrils.

The man fired at it and saw it fall, but as it was very dark he dared not go near it; but on the following morning he went to the spot and saw where it had fallen, by the marks of blood from its wound. Tracking it by this means he followed its path until it had reached a bridge, where the woman's tracks took the place of the dog's tracks in the path. He followed the bloody trail to the Tonawanda Reservation, where he found the woman. She had died from the effect of the shot.

A MAN WHO ASSUMED THE SHAPE OF A HOG.

On the Tonawanda Reservation three boys were coming down a hill, when they saw a large hog, which they concluded to follow to find its home. As they pursued the hog they continually kicked it, and it retaliated by biting at them at times. It retreated toward the bank of a small creek, reaching which it suddenly disappeared. They saw no reason to suppose that it had drowned itself in the stream ; but while searching for it they found on one of the banks an old man, who laughed and said, " What do you seek?" They answered, " A hog."

After some moments the old man said that it was he, himself, whom they had been chasing, and by this the boys knew that he was a witch.

WITCH TRANSFORMATION.

A Canadian Indian says he saw, one evening, on the road, a white bull with fire streaming from its nostrils, which, after it had passed him, he pursued. He had never seen so large a bull, or in fact any white bull, upon the reservation. As it passed in front of a house it was transformed into a man with a large white blanket, who was ever afterward known as a witch.

A SUPERSTITION ABOUT FLIES.

There was once a species of fly so poisonous that sometimes merely the smell of them would eat the nose from a man's face. A certain species of woodpecker was the only thing that could destroy them. Their homes were in trees, on which their poisonous tracks could be traced. They often entered the horns of a deer; hence, the Indian hunter's first move after shooting a deer was to examine its horns, and if they were infected, the hunter would run away, since he knew that the moment the animal died the fatal insect would emerge from the horn.

Around the trees in which they lived deer ever congregated, seemingly bewitched by these fierce and noxious little flies.

Buckskin and deerskin were used to catch them. The bird that killed them for food was colored black and yellow. In the evening it came forth from its home in a hollow tree and scoured the forests for them.

These birds were caught with buckskin traps and their feathers were used as charms, being fastened to the arrows of the hunter. An arrow thus made potent would surely bring down the deer.

CHAPTER IV.

MYTHOLOGIC EXPLANATION OF PHENOMENA.

The instinctive desire in man to fathom the mystery of human life, to solve the enigma of whence he came and whither he goes, and to account for the marvels ever presented to his senses, has in all times excited the imagination and originated speculation. To explain the phenomena of life and nature the untutored mind has seized upon every analogy suggesting the slightest clew, and imagination has aided the crude reasoning faculties.

In the numerous Iroquois myths relating to the origin of both animate and inanimate objects in nature there appears a reflex of the Indian's mind as he solves, to his entire satisfaction, mysteries, many of which are the " burning questions" of this enlightened age.

These tales only vary with the temperament of the narrator or the exigencies of the locality. Where oft repeated they have in time been recorded on the hearts and minds of the people either as myths or folk-lore, embodying the fossilized knowledge and ideas of a previous age, misinterpreted, perhaps, by those who have inherited them.

For the ethnologist who would trace in mythology the growth of the human mind, nowhere is the harvest more rich than among the aborigines of our own country; and prominent among these, in this lore of "faded metaphors", are the Iroquois. To what dignity their folk-lore might have attained had they been left to reach a lettered civilization for themselves we cannot know; but, judging from the history of other peoples, their first chroniclers would have accepted many of these oral traditions as facts.

To many from whom the writer received these myths they were realities, for there remain among these forest children those who still cling to their oft-told tales as the only link binding them to a happier past. Nor should they be considered as idle tales by the civilized man, who has not yet rid himself of the shackles of superstition in a thousand forms, and who sees daily his household gods torn down before him by comparative mythology and its allied sciences. Let him rather accept them reverently as the striving of the infant human mind in its search after the unknowable, revealing that inherent something in man which presupposes the existence of hidden forces, powers, or beings in nature. At first, perhaps, this is a mere blind feeling, but as man develops, it becomes an idea, then a recognized possibility; later, an article of religious faith.

ORIGIN OF THE HUMAN RACE.

The Iroquois legend of an origin of the human race, which includes the creation of the spirits of good and evil, is undoubtedly of modern origin.

In the great past, deep water covered all the earth. The air was filled with birds, and great monsters were in possession of the waters, when a beautiful woman was seen by them falling from the sky. Then huge ducks gathered in council and resolved to meet this wonderful creature and break the force of her fall. So they arose, and, with pinion overlapping pinion, unitedly received the dusky burden. Then the monsters of the deep also gathered in council to decide which should hold this celestial being and protect her from the terrors of the water, but none was able except a giant tortoise, who volunteered to endure this lasting weight upon his back. There she was gently placed, while he, constantly increasing in size, soon became a large island. Twin boys were after a time brought forth by the woman—one the spirit of good, who made all good things, and caused the maize, fruit, and tobacco to grow ; the other the spirit of evil, who created the weeds and all vermin. Ever the world was increasing in size, although occasional quakings were felt, caused by the efforts of the monster tortoise to stretch out, or by the contraction of his muscles.

After the lapse of ages from the time of his general creation Ta-rhu^n-hiă-wăh-ku^n, the Sky Holder, resolved upon a special creation of a race which should surpass all others in beauty, strength, and bravery; so from the bosom of the great island, where they had previously subsisted upon moles, Ta-rhu^n-hiă-wăh-ku^n brought out the six pairs, which were destined to become the greatest of all people.

The Tuscaroras tell us that the first pair were left near a great river, now called the Mohawk. The second family were directed to make their home by the side of a big stone. Their descendants have been termed the Oneidas. Another pair were left on a high hill, and have ever been called the Onondagas. Thus each pair was left with careful instructions in different parts of what is now known as the State of New York, except the Tuscaroras, who were taken up the Roanoke River into North Carolina, where Ta-rhu^n-hiă-wăh-ku^n also took up his abode, teaching them many useful arts before his departure. This, say they, accounts for the superiority of the Tuscaroras. But each of the six tribes will tell you that his own was the favored one with whom Sky Holder made his terrestrial home, while the Onondagas claim that their possession of the council fire prove them to have been the chosen people.

Later, as the numerous families became scattered over the State, some lived in localities where the bear was the principal game, and were called from that circumstance the clan of the Bear. Others lived where the beavers were trapped, and they were called the Beaver clan. For similar reasons the Snipe, Deer, Wolf, Tortoise, and Eel clans received their appellations.

FORMATION OF THE TURTLE CLAN.

The Turtle clan originated in a simple and straightforward fashion. There were in early times many tortoises of the kind familiarly known as mud turtles, inhabiting a small lake or pool. During a very hot summer this pool became dry. The turtles thereupon set out on their travels over the country to look for a new habitation. One of them, who was particularly fat, suffered a good deal from this unaccustomed exercise. After a time his shoulders became blistered under his shell from the effect of his exertions in walking, and he, finally, by an extraordinary effort, threw off his shell altogether. The process of transformation and development, thus commenced, went on, and in a short time this fat and lazy turtle became a man, who was the progenitor of the Turtle clan.

HOW THE BEAR LOST HIS TAIL.

The following was recounted to me on the "Six Nations Reserve" in Canada, by Ka-an-er-wah, one of the few surviving grandchildren of Brant, the Mohawk, and might be termed a modern Indian story. It accounts for the tailless condition of the bear.

A cunning fox saw a wagon load of fish and resorted to the following ruse to obtain some of the coveted delicacy: Feigning to be dead, he laid himself in the road by which the fisherman must pass, who, thinking the skin of the fox worth preserving, tossed him into his wagon and drove on. After throwing out several fish, the fox slyly crawled out himself. Soon he met a wolf who was informed of his good luck, and advised to try the same experiment. The fisherman had, in the mean time, discovered the trick, and the wolf received a good thrashing instead of a fish dinner.

The fox next met a bear who was also anxious to procure some fish. "Well," replied the fox, "down at the river you will find an air-hole in the ice; just put your tail down into it as I did and you can draw out the fish as fast as you wish." The bear followed the directions carefully, but, the weather being cold, instead of securing a fish his tail was frozen off.

The bear was very angry and proposed to fight a duel with the fox. The fox chose as his seconds a dog and a cat; the bear chose a hog, and awaited the fox at the appointed hour. As the latter was late in appearing the bear clambered into a tree to prospect, and reported that the fox was approaching with two men armed with guns. Thereupon the hog, greatly frightened, begged to be covered with leaves. Having accomplished this, the bear returned to his post in the tree.

The fox soon made his appearance, but instead of men his companions proved to be a dog and a lame cat. While awaiting in their turn, the cat, perceiving the slight motion of one of the uncovered ears of the hog, sprang upon it, whereupon the squeals of the invisible pig put the whole company to flight, and the bear never had the satisfaction of avenging the loss of his tail.

ORIGIN OF MEDICINE.

Chief Mt. Pleasant, one of the Bear clan, relates that once on a time a sickly old man, covered with sores, entered an Indian village where over each wigwam was placed the sign of the clan of its possessor; for instance, the beaver skin denoting the Beaver clan, the deer skin the Deer clan. At each of these wigwams the old man applied for food and a night's lodging, but his repulsive appearance rendered him an object of scorn, and the Wolf, the Tortoise, and the Heron had bidden the abject old man to pass on. At length, tired and weary, he arrived at a wigwam where a bear skin betokened the clanship of its owner. This he found inhabited by a kind-hearted woman who immediately refreshed him with food and spread out skins for his bed. Then she was instructed by the old man to go in search of certain herbs, which she prepared according to his directions, and through their efficacy he was soon healed. Then he commanded that she should treasure up this secret. A few days after, he sickened with a fever and again commanded a search for other herbs and was again healed. This being many times repeated he at last told his benefactress that his mission was accomplished, and that she was now endowed with all the secrets for curing disease in all its forms, and that before her wigwam should grow a hemlock tree whose branches should reach high into the air above all others, to signify that the Bear should take precedence of all other clans, and that she and her clan should increase and multiply.

ORIGIN OF WAMPUM.

A man while walking in a forest saw an unusually large bird covered with a heavily clustered coating of wampum. He immediately informed his people and chiefs, whereupon the head chief offered as a prize his beautiful daughter to one who would capture the bird, dead or alive, which apparently had come from another world. Whereupon the warriors, with bows and arrows, went to the "tree of promise," and as each lucky one barely hit the bird it would throw off a large quantity of the coveted coating, which, like the Lernæan hydra's heads, multiplied by being cropped. At last, when the warriors were despairing of success, a little boy from a neighboring tribe came to satisfy his curiosity by seeing the wonderful bird of which he had heard, but as his people were at war with this tribe he was not permitted by the warriors to try his skill at archery, and was even threatened with death. But the head chief said, " He is a mere boy; let him shoot on equal terms with you who are brave and fearless warriors." His decision being final, the boy, with unequaled skill, brought the coveted bird to the ground.

Having received the daughter of the head chief in marriage, he divided the oh-ko-äh between his own tribe and that into which he had married, and peace was declared between them. Then the boy husband decreed that wampum should be the price of peace and blood, which was adopted by all nations. Hence arose the custom of giving belts of wampum to satisfy violated honor, hospitality, or national privilege.

ORIGIN OF TOBACCO.

A boat filled with medicine men passed near a river bank, where a loud voice had proclaimed to all the inhabitants to remain indoors; but some, disobeying, died immediately. The next day the boat was sought for and found, containing a strange being at each end, both fast asleep. A loud voice was then heard saying that the destroying of these creatures would result in a great blessing to the Indian.

So they were decoyed into a neighboring council-house, where they were put to death and burned, and from their ashes rose the tobacco plant.

ORIGIN OF PLUMAGE.

In the beginning the birds, having been created naked, remained hidden, being ashamed of their nakedness. But at last they assembled in a great council and petitioned the gods to give them some kind of covering. They were told that their coverings were all ready, but were a long way off, and they must either go or send for them. Accordingly, another council was held to induce some bird to go in search of the plumage, but each had some excuse for not going. At last a turkey-buzzard volunteered to go and bring the feathery uniforms. It being a long journey to the place whence he must bring them, he (who had been a clean bird heretofore) was obliged to eat carrion and filth of all kinds; hence his present nature. At length, directed by the gods, he found the coverings, and selfishly appropriated to himself the most beautifully colored one, but finding he could not fly in this, he continued trying them on until he selected his present suit, in which, although it is the least beautiful of any, he can so gracefully ride through the air. The good turkey-buzzard then returned, bearing the feathery garments, from which each bird chose his present colored suit.

WHY THE CHIPMUNK HAS THE BLACK STRIPE ON HIS BACK.

Once upon a time the porcupine was appointed to be the leader of all the animals. Soon after his appointment he called them all together and presented the question, "Shall we have night all the time and darkness, or daylight with its sunshine?" This was a very important question, and a violent discussion arose, some wishing for daylight and the sun to rule, and others for continual night.

The chipmunk wished for night and day, weeks and months, and night to be separate from the days, so he began singing, "The light will come; we must have light," which he continued to repeat. Meanwhile the bear began singing, "Night is best; we must have darkness."

While the chipmunk was singing, the day began to dawn. Then the other party saw that the chipmunk was prevailing, and were very angry; and their leader, the bear, pursued the chipmunk, who managed to escape uninjured, the huge paw of the bear simply grazing his back as he entered his hole in a hollow tree, leaving its black imprint, which the chipmunk has ever since retained. But night and day have ever continued to alternate.

ORIGIN OF THE CONSTELLATIONS.

Iroquois tradition tells us that the sun and moon existed before the creation of the earth, but the stars had all been mortals or favored animals and birds.

Seven little Indian boys were once accustomed to bring at eve their corn and beans to a little mound, upon the top of which, after their feast, the sweetest of their singers would sit and sing for his mates who danced around the mound. On one occasion they resolved on a more sumptuous feast, and each was to contribute towards a savory soup. But the parents refused them the needed supplies, and they met for a feastless dance. Their heads and hearts grew lighter as they flew around the mound, until suddenly the whole company whirled off into the air. The inconsolable parents called in vain for them to return, but it was too late. Higher and higher they arose, whirling around their singer, until, transformed into bright stars, they took their places in the firmament, where, as the Pleiades, they are dancing still, the brightness of the singer having been dimmed, however, on account of his desire to return to earth.

A party of hunters were once in pursuit of a bear, when they were attacked by a monster stone giant, and all but three destroyed. The three together, with the bear, were carried by invisible spirits up into the sky, where the bear can still be seen, pursued by the first hunter with his bow, the second with the kettle, and the third, who, farther behind, is gathering sticks. Only in fall do the arrows of the hunters pierce the bear, when his dripping blood tinges the autumn foliage. Then for a time he is invisible, but afterwards reappears.

An old man, despised and rejected by his people, took his bundle and staff and went up into a high mountain, where he began singing the death chant. Those below, who were watching him, saw him slowly rise into the air, his chant ever growing fainter and fainter, until it finally ceased as he took his place in the heavens, where his stooping figure, staff, and bundle have ever since been visible, and are pointed out as Nǎ-gê-tci (the old man).

An old woman, gifted with the power of divination, was unhappy because she could not also foretell when the world would come to an end. For this she was transported to the moon, where to this day she is clearly to be seen weaving a forehead-strap. Once a month she stirs the boiling kettle of hominy before her, during which occupation the cat, ever by her side, unravels her net, and so she must continue until the end of time, for never until then will her work be finished.

As the pole star was ever the Indian's guide, so the northern lights were ever to him the indication of coming events. Were they white, frosty weather would follow; if yellow, disease and pestilence; while red predicted war and bloodshed: and a mottled sky in the springtime was ever the harbinger of a good corn season.

THE POLE STAR.

A large party of Indians, while moving in search of new hunting grounds, wandered on for many moons, finding but little game. At last they arrived. at the banks of a great river, entirely unknown to them, where they had to stop, not having the material to build boats. Lost and nearly famished with hunger, the head chief was taken very ill, and it was decided to hold a council to devise means for returning to their old homes. During the dance, and while the tobacco was burning, a little being like a child came up, saying she was sent to be their guide. Accordingly they broke up their camp and started with her that night. Preceding them, with only a gi-wǎh, or small war-club, she led them on until daylight and then commanded them to rest while she prepared their food. This they did, and when awakened by her they found a great feast in readiness for them. Then she bade them farewell, with the assurance of returning to them again in the evening.

True to her word, at evening she reappeared, bringing with her a skin jug, from which she poured out some liquid into a horn cup, and bade them each to taste of it. At first they feared to do so, but at last yielding they began to feel very strong. She then informed them that they had a long journey to make that night. Again they followed her, and in the early morn arrived at a great plain, where she bade them rest again for the day, with the exception of a few warriors who were to be shown where they could fine plenty of game. Two of the warriors had accompanied her but a short distance when they encountered a herd of deer, of which she bade them kill all they wished in her absence, and then, again promising to return at night, she took leave of them. At night-fall she returned, saying her own chief would soon follow her to explain to them how they could reach their own homes in safety. In a short time he arrived, with a great number of his race, and immediately all held council together and informed the Indians that they were now in the territory of the pigmies, who would teach them a sign, already in the sky, which would be to them a sure guide whenever they were lost; and the pigmies pointed out the pole star and told them that in the north, where the sun never goes, while other stars moved about, this particular star should stand still, as the Indian's guide in his wanderings, and that they were then but to follow its light and they would soon return to their tribe, where they would find plenty of game, &c.

Then they thanked the good pigmies, and traveled every night until they arrived safely in their homes, where, when they had recounted all their adventures, the head chief called a meeting of all the tribes and said they ought to give this star a name. So they called it ti-yn-sōu-dă-go-êrr (the star which never moves), by which name it is called unto this day.

CHAPTER V.

TALES.

Distinct from the myths, which relate to the gods, supernatural beings, and natural phenomena, are the tales, from which must be gleaned hints regarding the past hunter, warrior, and family life and history of the Iroquois.

In time of peace, during the long winter evenings, among his group of friends, the returned hunter narrated his achievements, or some famous story-teller told of those days in the past when men and animals could transform themselves at will and hold converse with one another. If musical, the entertainer would relate ingenious fables, with songs introduced, to give zest to the narration.

All these historical traditions, legends of war and hunting, fairy tales, and fables have been handed down through the ages, kindling the enthusiasm of the marvel-loving listener.

These story-tellers were gifted with such imaginative powers, and were so free from the trammels of adapting their tales to any standard of possibility, that no easy task lies before the careful student who seeks to detect in them the scaffolding of truth around which so elaborate a superstructure has been reared.

BOY RESCUED BY A BEAR.

From their close relations with wild animals Indians' stories of transformations of men into beasts and beasts into men are numerous and interesting. In nearly all of these, wherever the bear is introduced he figures as a pattern of benevolence, while many other animals, such as the porcupine, are always presented as noxious. One of these bear stories, as told me on the Cattaraugus Reservation by a grandson of Cornplanter, was as follows: A party of hunters, who were encamped a long distance from home, discovered, as they were preparing to return, that a young boy of their company was missing. After searching vainly for several days they concluded that he had been killed, and sadly departed without him. They were no sooner gone, however, than the lost child, in an almost famishing condition, was discovered by a very kind-hearted bear, who reasoned thus: "If I attempt to relieve the child in my present form, he will surely be frightened to death. I will therefore transform myself into a woman and take the boy home with me to become a playmate for my little cubs." The boy was accordingly rescued from starvation, and, living in the same hollow tree with the bear family, fed with them upon nuts, corn, and berries. But when fall came, and with it the return of the hunters, the good bear explained her device to the boy, saying: "My cubs must now take care of themselves, and you can rejoin your friends; but always feel kindly toward the bear tribe"; upon which she resumed her proper shape and disappeared into the woods. The boy never, even when grown, was known to kill a bear.

INFANT NURSED BY BEARS.

A man and his wife and child went off hunting from an Indian village and encamped a long way from home. At first, good luck attended the hunter, who brought into camp plenty of deer and other game. At last, game became scarce, and day after day the hunter returned empty-handed and famishing with hunger. Before leaving, the hunter resolved to try his luck once more. Soon after he had left the camp his wife, in searching for roots, found a hole in a large tree in which was a black bear. This she succeeded in killing, and after cutting it up and cooking some for herself and child she carefully secreted the remainder from her husband. But the boy hid a piece for his father, who soon returned, very weary. Then the hunter was enraged at the conduct of his wife, whom he forced to eat of the meat until she died, with her little infant to which she had given birth the same hour.

Then the hunter buried his wife and threw the infant into the hollow tree. After this the hunter had better luck, and continued to live in the same place with his little boy. In the course of time he found that his little son must have had company, for little foot-prints were to be seen around his wigwam. So he left a second small bow and arrow, which, in time, he found had been used, and his son told him that a small boy had been playing with him. The next day the father watched and saw a little boy leave the tree where he had placed what he supposed to be the dead child. Then he entered his home and said to the child, "You are my child"; but the boy could not understand him, and was frightened and uneasy, and ran away to the tree, where the hunter discovered he had been nourished and cared for by a friendly bear. The hunter would not kill the kind benefactor, but took some of the soft bed of dried bark, to which the child had been accustomed, to his home, whereupon the child was happy and contented to remain with his father and brother.

In time the two excelled in hunting and brought home owls and strange birds. Finally, they told their father they were going to the far west to kill the great beasts which were harming the human race. The hunter, who perceived that the children were becoming very strange, was afraid of them and consented. Then they bade him go back to his native home and get three of the bravest warriors to follow them to the west, where the warriors would find the carcasses of the animals which they would kill. So he went home and told his story, and the warriors started out and finally found traces of the boys, and in time found the carcasses of the animals almost reduced to bones. Two of the men died of the stench.

THE MAN AND HIS STEP-SON.

This tale was narrated by a granddaughter of Brant.

A certain man had a step-son whom he hated. He devised all means of getting rid of him. At last an idea struck him. He went out hunting very often, and one day he saw a porcupine's hole. " The very thing," said he. When he came home he called his step-son. " See here," said he, " I have found a porcupine's nest. I want you to creep into the hole and catch some of the young ones. Come, crawl in." The boy obeyed, and as soon as his heels were in, the step-father closed up the hole and made him a prisoner.

When he had found himself betrayed he cried and cried till he cried himself asleep. When he awakened he found that he was in a room. He saw an old woman walking around. She brought him something to eat, but it was so bitter that he refused. Then she called many animals around her to a council—wolves, bears, foxes, and deer. She told them that there was a boy there who could not eat the food that she lived on, and asked what they would advise to give which might support a human being? The fox said, " I live on geese and fowls. I'll take him, but still he can't eat raw food."

The council decided that it was useless for him to assume the charge.

Then the deer and each animal in turn told what they lived upon, but none could offer proper food for a lad.

Last of all the bear spoke. " I live," said he, " on nuts, and he can live with my young ones." So this was agreed to. All the animals promised to assist in getting the nuts, and the boy was given over to the keeping of the bear. He kept him for several years. One day the bear said, " A hunter is coming; he means to chop down the tree."

True enough, next day a dog ran barking up, and the tree was cut down and the old bear and two cubs were killed.

The hunter thought there might be still another cub, so he looked into the tree. The boy made a noise just like the cubs. The hunter caught him, and was so astonished at his appearance that, instead of killing him, he took him to his wigwam, tamed him, and taught him to speak and to grow up like a man. After some years he forgot he had lived like a bear. He married a daughter of the hunter, but his mother-in-law was always angry because he never brought home tender bear-meat. So at last he went hunting and killed a bear, but on his return home he fell on a sharp stick and was instantly killed.

THE BOY AND HIS GRANDMOTHER.

An old woman lived with her grandson in the wilderness. The boy amused himself by shooting with his bow and arrows, and was very happy. His grandmother cooked and cleaned. She talked much to him of the future and the time when he should go out into the world. "Never, my grandson," she would say, "never go west—go always to the east." And the boy wondered very much at this, because, he said, all other boys went west, and they found much game there. But he promised.

However, one day he asked his grandmother so often why she always forbade him to go west, that she told him: "Far away in the west," said she, "there lives one who waits to destroy us, and if he sees you he will injure you and me. I warn you do not go that way." But the boy questioned how and why, and thought to himself that on the first opportunity he would see for himself. So he struck out for the west, keeping a sharp lookout for the man, because his grandmother had taught him he should always bow first.

As he neared the lake he heard the man's voice, but, although he looked all around, he could see no one. The voice said: "Ah! ah! my little fellow, I see you." Still he could see no one. "What shall I do now?" thought he. Then the voice said, "What would you think if I sent a hurricane to tear your grandmother's cabin all up?" The boy replied, "Oh, I should like it. We have hard work to get wood. It would be a good thing." And the voice replied, "You had better run home and see." So he went home to his grandmother. As he neared his cabin he heard a great noise, and his grandmother called to him, "Come in, come in; we shall be blown away. You have disobeyed me; now we shall be destroyed. The hurricane is upon us." But the boy only laughed and said, "We will throw the house into a rock." And he turned it into a rock, and when the hurricane was over they were unharmed, and found plenty of wood to burn.

Then said the boy, "Grandmother, we are all right." But the old woman said, "Do not venture any more; next time he will destroy us." But the lad thought he would try again. In the morning he started off east as long as his grandmother could see him, then he turned to the west, and kept a sharp watch right and left as he neared the pond. Then, all at once, he heard the man's voice again. "What," it asked, "would you say if a great hailstorm came down upon your mother's cabin, with spears as sharp as needles?" "Oh," replied the youngster, "I have always wanted some spears; I would be glad of some." "You had better go home and see," said the voice. So home he sped, hearing the gathering of a great storm.

The grandmother said, "We are going to be destroyed with a hailstorm of spears." But he laughed aloud and said, "I need spears for fishing; let them come. We will turn the house into a rock again."

And he did, and when the storm was ended he and his grandmother came out and the ground was covered with spears. "No matter," said he; "I will get poles and fit them on for fishing"; but when he brought the pole he could not find any spears. "How is this?" he asked. And his grandmother said, "They are melted—they were ice."

The boy was very much disappointed and mourned aloud. "What can I do to punish the old fellow?" he cried. "Heed my warning," said his grandmother, "and leave him alone."

But the lad was determined. He started off once more, taking with him a stone round his neck as a charm. He watched the direction in which he had heard the voice, and all at once he saw in the middle of the lake a great head, with a face on every side of it. He cried out, "Ha! ha! uncle, I have you now. How should you like it if the lake dried up?" "That it will never do," said the voice. "Go home," mocked the lad, "and see!" And he threw the stone which he had. As it whirled through the air it became very large and fell into the lake, when, at once, the water began to boil.

Then the boy returned to his grandmother's cabin and told her all about it. She said, "It has been tried again and again, but no one has ever seen him before or has been able to hunt him."

Next morning he went over to the lake and found it all dried up and all the animals dead, and only a large frog remained, into which the man had been turned. So the boy killed the frog, and no more trouble ever came to him or his grandmother.

THE DEAD HUNTER.

A man and his wife went hunting, and after a hard day's march they came to an empty wigwam. So they entered and found in it a dead man, laid out with his tomakawk and all his fine things. They found corn in plenty, and the squaw made bread, and then they all went to bed, the man on one side and the woman and her baby on the other. They placed some of the bread between them, and in the middle of the night they heard a noise, and the dead man was sitting up and eating. The hunter sprang up. "We are all dead folks," cried he, "if we remain here"; so he made a pretense, and whispered to the squaw, "You must go for water. I will mind the child." As soon as she was gone, he pinched the baby till it cried. "Oh," said he, "I must follow the mother or the child will die; she is too long fetching the water." He hastened and soon caught up with the woman, but behind him came the dead man, holding a lighted torch. To save themselves they put the child down on the ground, and the hunter seized his wife's hand and hurried her on faster and faster, but the sound of steps behind them was plainer and plainer. So the man let his wife go, and fled on by himself as hard as he could. Soon he came to a hollow log, into which he crept. The steps came nearer and nearer, until at last he felt the strokes of the dead man's hatchet, and heard the dead man's voice saying, "Ah! you are here. I have caught you." Then the dead man took a pole and tried to poke the hunter out of the hollow, but he could not. At last his hatchet broke, and then the hunter heard him say, " I must go; my night is coming on." So, after a while, the hunter crept out of the hollow log and went after his wife and child, and returned to the settlement and told all about it; and the chief sent and burnt up the dead man's wigwam until it was nothing but ashes.

A HUNTER'S ADVENTURES.

This was told by Mr. Snow, Seneca Reservation:

A hunter far from home had expended all of his arrows, when he arrived at a lake. He saw a great number of wild geese. Having been unsuccessful, he now reflected upon the best means of capturing some of these geese, and he finally concluded to pursue the following plan: He procured a quantity of second-growth bass-wood bark, which he tore into withes. These he fastened to his belt, then, swimming out into the lake, he dove down under the floating flock and succeeded in tying a few of the geese to his belt, whereupon the struggling geese, with their companions, flew up into the air, carrying the hunter with them. While unfastening a few of the tied ones, so that he might be let down to the ground in a gradual manner, the whole of the captured ones broke away, and the poor hunter fell into a tall and hollow stump, from which he found it impossible to free himself.

He remained in this miserable prison nearly two days, when he with joy heard a thumping sound upon the outside of the stump, and also the voices of women choppers, who were cutting down the stump for wood, but the cries of the man on the inside of the stump frightened the women so much that they went away in search of aid to secure the game which they supposed they had found in the stump.

The hunter was finally delivered safely from his perilous situation, and he remained with his kind rescuers until he had again provided himself with a large stock of arrows, when he started anew for a hunt farther to the south. Having arrived at his destination, he built a lodge and had excellent luck in killing large numbers of deer, bears, and other game, the oil of which he carefully preserved in leathern bottles. When he concluded to return to his home and friends he remembered his experience in flying, so he prepared wings for himself, which wings he made from thinly-dressed deer-skin. Taking his bottles of oil for ballast, he started homeward, but as he passed over the lodges of the good women who had rescued him, he threw down several bottles to these his good friends, who to this day do not know from whence they came. After

this the flying hunter flew swiftly and safely to his home. His return to his clan was announced by runners, and all assembled to listen to the hunter's narration of his exploits and adventures.

THE OLD MAN'S LESSONS TO HIS NEPHEW.

A man and his nephew lived together in a solitary place. The old man one day said to his nephew, "You are now a young man. You should be hunting larger game—a bear or a deer—for our support." And he replied, "I will go." Then the old man gave him the best bow and arrows, and in the morning he departed. When he returned home he brought that which he had killed—a deer—and thought himself lucky for a first attempt. "I should like," he said to his uncle, "to go every day." Then the old man said, "Now and again you may see a bear go up a tree; if you see a hole in the tree and the marks of the bear's claws you can be sure of the bear."

So one day as the young man was out he saw a hole in a tree, and he saw the claw marks of the bear, showing that he had gone up, so he returned and told his uncle, and in the morning they started together. The old man said, "I believe there is a bear inside now. Our plan is to knock around the outside of the tree and make the bear uneasy; presently he will come out." So they knocked, and the first thing they knew the bear was sticking his head out of the hole. "Now," said the uncle, "I will tell you when to shoot. If you will shoot just where there is no hair, you will surely kill him." The young man saw that the paws were without hair and he hit the bear on the fore-paw. "Shoot again," said the uncle. So he shot the other paw. Then the old man pointed and said, "Shoot here." And the nephew aimed and shot the point of his uncle's finger. Then the old man's hand hurt him, so to direct his nephew he pursed out his lips and pointed with them, and the young man shot through his lips. Then the bear came down and made his way off, while the uncle was explaining that his meaning had been to shoot under the fore legs. The young man asked, "Why did you not say so?" Then they started home for that day without game. "To-morrow morning," said the uncle, "watch, for if you will look between the roots of the large trees you may find a bear in that way."

Accordingly, the next day the young man found a hole near the root of the tree and saw a large bear inside. So he went home and asked his uncle for instructions how to get at the bear. The old man began to explain, but, unfortunately, in a way that he could not understand. He went into the corn field, gathered the corn-stalks and stuck them around the entrance to the hole, so that he surrounded the place where the bear must come out. Then he knocked on the other side of the tree, and the bear came out, as, of course, there was no reason why he should not, for the stalks fell before him. The young man took his arms and went home. Then the uncle asked what he had done, and he told. "You did not understand," said the old man. "You should have shot him as he left the den; first on one side then on the other." "After this," expostulated the young man, "make your explanations clearer and do not give so many illustrations. Had you told me this at first all would have been right."

One day the old man said, "I'm going to make a feast. You can invite the guests. I cut sticks to represent so many friends. You invite them. Go to the highest tree you can find and leave this stick there. Then go along till you find a place all swamp—bad place, and leave one stick there," &c.

So the nephew went around and used up the sticks and returned. "Have you done as I said?" asked the old man. "Yes," said he. Yet when the day came and the feast was ready, nobody came. "Why," asked the uncle, "has nobody come?" "How," inquired the young man, "could the tall tree and the swamp come here?" So they ate together, and then the young fellow went off in the world to learn his lessons by experience, for he had become tired of his uncle's parables.

THE HUNTER AND HIS FAITHLESS WIFE.

Once on a time there was a man whose name was "Hemlock Bows." He used to go hunting every day and always had good luck. He would kill so many deer that he could not carry them all home. One day he killed thirty deer. He was determined to carry them all home, so he took them and shook them, and shook, and shook, till they were as small as squirrels, and he carried them all home, and when he got there he shook, and shook, and shook, till they were good-sized deer again. Sometimes when he killed so many he would sit up all night to fix the skins on his wigwam so he could make clothes for himself and his children. One day a boy was born unto him; the father was very fond of him and he planted a few hills of corn and beans, but they lived mostly on meat. After the child was born the mother slept alone with it on the other side of the fire-place.

After three years more a little girl was born. After the birth of her second child the wife seemed to care no more for her husband. He was a great worker. He had a large boxful of skins all dressed for his children.

When the father went hunting the mother would call the boy and make him go and bring her some water, and she would wash and dress up very fine and take a long strap and an ax and leave the children alone all day until almost time for the father to come home. Then she would hurry home to cook for the man.

One night the little boy told his father all about his mother going away every day. He felt very badly when he heard it, and at once resolved to follow her the next day and find where she went. The next morning early he left the cabin and went off. The woman soon sent the boy for some water, and, after she had dressed, started with her ax and the long strap which was used in drawing wood. She passed her husband on her way but did not see him, but he tracked her very closely. Soon she came to a large black-ash tree, which was hollow, and upon which she pounded with her ax. A very nice-looking man came out of the tree to meet her. He wore a turban filled with bright feathers. He went up to her and kissed her, and seemed very much delighted to see her. Her husband was watching them all the time, and when the man kissed her he drew his bow and arrow and shot at the man, and the arrow went between him and the woman. She was very angry, and took a club and beat her husband till he could not see. Then she went home, put the boy and girl out in the cold and snow, and then set fire to the cabin and burned it down and went off.

Soon the father came and found the children. He felt very badly when he saw them, but he told the boy he must mind the dog, for he must go after their mother. The dog fixed the boy and girl in a house in the snow, and the next day they started on a long walk. While the boy was traveling along with his little sister on his back she saw a flock of large white turkeys, and she wanted one. The boy put her down and ran in the bushes to find one for the little girl, but while he was after it a bear came and carried off the little girl, and the dog followed after the bear. The boy felt very bad. He cried and cried, and wished that he might die. He tried to hang himself, but the strap broke. Then he jumped down a steep place onto a lot of stones, but still he was unhurt. He traveled on and soon came to a lake. He plunged into the water, but it was very shallow. He walked a little way, when he saw a great fish coming towards him with its great mouth wide open. Now, not far from this lake lived a woman and her daughter. They had fences of osier fixed in the lake to catch fish. In the morning the girl went out to see if there were any fish caught, and she saw a very large one. They killed and dressed it, and when they cut it up there they found the boy alive. They were very glad to find the boy, and soon he told them all about himself and family.

Some time after this they heard that the boy's mother was going to be married to another man. The woman told the boy she thought he had better go and kill the man and his mother. So they fixed him up and he went and found them. There was a number of cabins and between two of them was a long stick put up, and on it was an eagle, and the one that shot the eagle was to marry the woman. She was very nicely dressed and sat on a raised platform. He saw his father near her, looking very sick and sad. The boy went around among the wigwams, and in one he found his sister hanging to a crane in a chimney and near her the dog. He got his father, sister, and dog away, and then went back and set fire to the cabin his mother was in. It burned so fast that she could not get out and she died. When her head cracked open it shook the ground, and out of the ashes of his mother there rose up a screech owl. His father got well, and they all went to live with the woman and her daughter. The old man married the woman, and the boy the daughter, and so they were happy at last.

THE CHARMED SUIT.

An old man brought up his son very quietly in a solitary place. As he grew up, his father sent him daily into the woods and told him to listen and come home and tell what he had heard. So the boy sat on a log and waited to hear what might come. He heard a sound at last, "Ch-R-Ch," so he ran to tell the old man and then thought he would wait till he heard it again. The Ch-R-Ch was repeated, and he ran to his home and cried out, "I have heard it! I have heard it!" "Wait! wait!" said the old man, "till I get my pipe," and when he had lifted it he said, "Now, what did you hear?" "Oh," replied the lad, "I heard Ch-R-Ch; twice it was repeated." "That," said the father "is not what I wanted you to hear; that was only a snow-bird."

So the boy went, morning after morning, and heard various sounds from snow-birds, wolves, owls, &c., but still never what the old man expected. One day whilst he was listening he heard quite a new sound and as the sun began to rise, it was like a voice singing. "That is strange" said he, "I never heard that before." The song was like this :

> Hă-hûm-weh
> Hă-hûm-weh
> Wă-he-dŭm-nä
>   Srû-guă he.
> Hă hûm weh
> Hă hûm weh.

Which means :

> I belong to the wolf clan.
> I belong to the wolf clan.
> I am going to marry him,
> I am going to marry him.

It was a sweet woman's voice. So the boy listened and said to himself, "Surely this is the song." So he shouted for glee, and ran and fell near the door, he was so excited. "Now," he cried, "I bring the news"; but the father said, "Wait! wait! till I get my pipe." "Now," said he, as he smoked, "tell me." So the boy began. "As I listened," said he, "I heard a voice from the west, a woman's voice, so I turned and listened to it singing":

> Hă-hûm-weh
> Wă-he-dûm-nä
> Srû-guă-hi.

"Ah!" said the father, "that was what I was waiting for. The chief of a distant village sends his two daughters to see us. Run half way back and see if you can hear them again." So he went and heard again the same song.

Hă-hûm-weh, &c.

He returned at once and told his uncle. "Now," said the old man, "they are almost here. Sit down by the ashes." And he took the shovel and threw ashes all over the boy's bed and put on him his best feathers and astonished the boy very much by saying, "Do not look at the maidens when they come in; they come to see me, not you; hold your head down while they stay."

Then they heard the song:

Hă-hûm-weh.
Hă-hûm-weh.
Srû-gnă-he.

The feathers were all on his head; still the old man repeated, "Now, keep still."

Soon the maidens arrived and the old man opened the door. The younger of the two carried a beautiful basket on her back; this she set down near the old man. The boy looked around a little, and his father called out, "Dirty boy; hold your head down." The visitors looked around and thought, "What a place! what a place!" "Sit down, sit down," said the old man to the visitors, but although they removed the blankets they stood still. So he smoked on quietly.

When they saw how dirty it was where the boy sat they began to go around and clear up, and as the evening passed the lad did not know what to do with himself. They fixed themselves a clean bed on the other side of the wigwam. They refused to sit by the old man, and when at last the boy went to sleep they lifted him out of his dirty bed, strewn with ashes, and put him into their clean bed.

In the morning the younger one admired him and said, "What a beautiful young man!" Then they said, "We had better cook something." So they cooked corn and rice, and the boy ate with them, and the old father smoked. After a while he said, "Good woman; can clean up, can cook, can make good wife." Then he let the boy look up. The younger visitor sang again:

Hă-hûm-weh.
Hă-hûm-weh.

So the old man smoked his pipe and the sisters went back to their people. Then the two lived quietly together, but the young man often thought of the beautiful maidens.

One day as they were conversing the old man said, "Now you have become a young man you must go." "Which way," asked he, and the uncle replied, "You must go where those young maidens are who are chief's daughters. You must have fine bows and arrows; here they are— try them before you go. They give luck in hunting." Then he looked where he kept all the fine things for the young warriors and dressed him up well with a swan stuffed. "Now," said he, "when you take this outside it will be on your head, but it will soon come back to life, and when that happens you must run in a circle and return, and you will see that many deer and bears will follow your track." So off he went. When he returned he said that so many bears and so many deer came out every time as he crossed the track and he shot them, and took the best out and sent them home to show them to the old man. And all the time the swan was alive and beautiful.

The old man exclaimed at his luck as he told his tale. "You have done well," said his uncle. "We must save all the meat. Now, hold yourself ready to go to-morrow. I warn you there are dangers in your path. There is a stream that you must cross. There stands a man and he will try to kill you. He will call out to you that he has a couple of wild cats and will say, 'My friend, come, help me kill these.' Pay no attention; go right on along, or you will be in danger and never get to the town." The nephew promised to obey, and his uncle brought out a curious thing, made of colored string and elk hair of deep red, about a foot long. "I shall keep this by me," said he, "and so long as you are doing well it will hang as it is; but if you are in danger it will come down itself almost to the ground, and if it does reach the ground you will die." "I will be careful," said the young man, and so he started with his directions, following his uncle's advice. He had almost reached his destination when he heard a noise, and there in his path stood a man while he watched two animals going up a tree, and he tried in vain to make them come down. As the young man approached him he said, "Please help me, if you can; but kill one of these animals; it will be a good thing. Do help me." So he begged, and the young man thought it could do no harm, so he took out his arrow and said, "Don't be in a hurry." Then the old man handed him the arrows and asked him, "Where are you going?" and he told him; and the stranger said, "Stop all night with me; that is a long way you are going; go on to-morrow."

Now the uncle at home was watching the signal. He saw it go down almost to the ground, and he cried out in his alarm, "Oh! oh! my nephew is in danger, he will get into trouble with that old man." But the young man listened to the persuasions of the tempter and agreed to remain with him all night, and the old man made up a fire and began to tell stories as they sat beside it till the youth fell asleep. Before they sat down he had gathered together some sharp prickly bark, pretending it gave a good light, and as the young man slept he said to himself, "Now, I can fix him." So he took some of the sharp-pointed bark and placed it on him; so he writhed in agony. Then he took off the young man's handsome clothes and dressed him up instead in his own old rags, dirty and rotten. "I shall keep these things," said he; "they are mine," and forthwith he started off to the chief's house where the beautiful women were, and he had the young man's pipe and his spotted deer skin, and the handsome bag made out of it, with little birds to light the pipe. When he reached the chief's cabin he went in and the younger sister was there. She was so disappointed when she saw him, she said, "This cannot be the young man." But her elder sister said: "Yes, it is he. He has the fine clothes and the deer skin, and the deer-skin bag, and the little birds to light his pipe." But still the younger sister was disappointed, and then the people heard that the young man they expected had come from the east and many came to see him and watched all his movements. At length he got his pipe, which, when it was filled, the two little birds were expected to light, but they would not for a stranger, so he said it was because there were people all around, and he must be alone. The older sister believed him. Then he told her, too: "When I spit it makes wampum, so spread out a deer skin and save my spittle." So he spat many times and she did as he said and saved it up, but it never became wampum, although he did it every night. Each day he went hunting, but he killed only things not good to eat, and made the older sister, who became his wife, cook them. The younger one, however, would never go near him. Even when he commanded the little spotted deer-skin bag to stand up she observed that it did not obey him.

One day she went out to the fields to husk corn, and as she finished her task she observed a man near a fire in the field. She drew near. He was fast asleep. She gazed at his face and recognized the beautiful young man, but how greatly changed! She stood for a while looking at him till he awakened. "Who are you?" she asked; "whence do you come? where are you going?" "I come," said he, "from the far east; I came only last evening." And he related his story, and told how nicely he had been started by his uncle, until she was quite satisfied of the truth of his story. She did not tell him she was the daughter of the chief whom he sought, but she went home and fetched food for him. She laid meat and drink before him, and while he ate she returned to her task of husking corn. Then she went home. The old fellow meanwhile had asked often, "Where is the young sister? Why does she never come to see me, or sit near whilst I smoke my pipe? May be she has found for herself a sickly man out in the field."

At last the younger sister told the young man who she was, and that the old man that had robbed him was in the chief's cabin and had all his fine things; and the young man felt better, and said, "I want my things back. I will make a dream. Go and tell the chief, your father, that I have dreamed a dream and all the people must come to hear it, and I will tell how all the things the old man has are mine, and then the birds will obey, and all the things will come alive again."

Then the old chief listened to the entreaties of his youngest daughter, and called a great council and the young man told his story in the form of a dream, and when he spoke of the birds they came and filled his pipe, and the swan skin when placed upon his head also came to life, and his spittle became wampum. So the chief knew he was the rightful owner of the clothes and they were returned to him, and the impostor was obliged to resume his old rags. The young man was then married to the faithful maiden, and returned to his home in safety, where he became in time a noted chief.

THE BOY AND THE CORN.

An old man brought up his nephew in a solitary place. One day as they walked through the field the uncle picked an ear of corn, but he did not eat it. " Strange," thought the boy, " that I never see him eating anything;" and he watched him when the old man thought he was asleep. He saw him go to a hole and take out a kettle and a few grains of corn, which he put into it. Then he took a magic wand and tapped the kettle till it grew big; then he ate some corn and again tapped the kettle till it became small once more.

In the morning when the uncle left home the boy got at the hole and did as he had seen him do, but as he tapped the kettle it grew so large that he could not stop it, and it went on growing until his uncle came home, who was very angry. "You do not know what harm you have been doing," said he ; " we can get no more corn; it grows in a place that is so dangerous that few who go there come back alive." " We have plenty in the house," said the boy. "And when it is gone, what then ?" But the boy persisted that he knew where the corn grew, and could easily fetch some. " So, uncle," he added, " tell me how to proceed." " I shall never see you again," moaned the uncle. " Oh, yes, you will," said the boy, and he started. Now, the uncle had warned him that he would come to a lake where the woman witches lived, and that he never could escape them. But he made himself a canoe and picked some peculiar nuts and launched himself upon the water. Then he threw the nuts before him to feed the fowls who guarded the shore, that they might not betray his coming. He landed on the other side safely and filled his pockets with corn, and was hastening to put off in his boat, but before he did so was curious to know what was in a lodge on the shore. So he peeped in and stole a bear's leg which he saw.

Now, all his nuts were gone; so when he passed the birds they were alarmed and set up their call and out came the witches with their hooks and cords. But he launched his canoe, and when a hook reached him he broke it off, and reached the opposite shore in safety. There he saw a number of ducks, and he stripped a tree of its bark and caught them and started home. As he neared his home he heard his uncle singing a dirge—"My poor nephew, I shall never see him again." The animals had been telling the old man sad tales of his death, so when the boy knocked at the door he did not believe that it was his nephew. But the boy heard the Hi-Wadi, and he knew his uncle. So he said, "Uncle,

I am coming, I am coming; stop your mourning." His uncle thought
it was an animal on the outside, and he called out, "Put your hand
through the hole." So the nephew put his hand through and caught
hold of the rope and pulled it out and tied it to a post, and then opened
the door. And when the old man saw his nephew he called out, "So
you have got home safe; where have you been?" and he made many
inquiries. And the young man explained everything to him, and told
how, at last, he had returned safely to his home with plenty of corn.

THE LAD AND THE CHESTNUTS.

This is another version of the foregoing tale:

A man lived with his younger brother alone in the deep wilderness. Game was plentiful—very plentiful. The elder brother hunted
it; the younger staid home to gather sticks and build the fire against
the hunter's return. When he came, bringing deer, the younger one
said, "I will cook the venison; give it to me to prepare for supper."
The elder one replied, "I will smoke before I eat." When he had
smoked he went to lie down. "I should think," said the younger,
"you would want to eat now." But no, he slept instead of tasting the
food, and when he awakened he bade his brother go to bed, and leave
him to help himself.

The lad wondered, but he obeyed. Still he found the same thing
happened every day. In the mornings the elder brother left without
eating; in the evenings he bade the boy leave him alone. This awakened the curiosity of the younger. "I will watch," said he; and he
watched. "He must eat something," he added to himself, "or he would
die. He must eat at night." So he pretended to take no notice. At
bedtime he lay down and made believe to sleep, but he kept one eye
open, although he seemed to be sound asleep.

After a while the elder brother rose and opened a trap-door, and, when
below the ground, he began to make strange motions, and presently
drew out a kettle and commenced scraping it on the bottom. Then he
poured water onto it, and at last he took a whip and struck the kettle,
saying, as he placed it over the burning wood, "Now, my kettle will
grow larger"; and as he struck it, it became bigger with every blow;
and at length it was very large, and he set it to cool, and began greedily
to eat the contents. "Ah," thought the younger brother, as he watched,
"now, to-morrow, I will find out what he eats;" and he went to sleep
content.

At daylight the elder set off to hunt. Now was the opportunity.
Cautiously the boy lifted the trap-door, and there he at once saw the
kettle. In it lay half a chestnut. "Now I know," said he, "what my
brother eats;" and he thought to himself, "I will fix it all ready for him

before he comes back." As night drew on he took the kettle and scraped up the chestnut, put in some water, and found the stick. He at once commenced whipping the kettle as he had seen his brother do, saying, "Now my kettle will grow large;" and it did; but it kept on growing larger and larger, to his surprise, until it filled the whole room, and he had to go up on the roof to stir it from the outside.

When the elder brother returned he said, "What are you doing?" "I found the kettle," replied the younger, "and was getting your supper." "Woe is me," said the elder, "now I must die." He struck and struck the kettle, and reduced it by every blow, until at last he could restore it to its place. But he was sorrowful. When morning came he would not get up, nor eat of the venison, but asked for his pipe and smoked.

Day by day passed. He grew weaker each day, and after each smoke sang, "Hah geh-he geh, Non ta ge je ō dah!" "Bring me my pipe and let me die."

The younger lad was very anxious. "Where," he asked his brother, "did you get the chestnuts? Let me go and seek some for you." After many questions at length the brother said, "Far, far away is a large river, which it is almost impossible to cross. On the further side, at a great distance, stands a house; near it is a tree, a chestnut tree; there my forefathers gathered chestnuts long ago, but now none can reach it, for there stands night and day a white heron watching the tree and looking around on every side. He is set there by the women folks; half a dozen of them take care of him, and for them he watches. If he hears a sound he makes his Thr-hr-hr. Then the women come out with war-clubs and are always on their guard lest any one should gather the chestnuts, as many fall on the ground. Even a mouse is suspected of being a man. There is no chance, no chance at all." But the brother said, "I must go and try this for your sake; I cannot have you die."

So he departed on his way, after he had made a little canoe about three inches long. He walked on and on, day and night, until at last he reached the river. Then he took out of his pouch his little canoe, and drew it out and out until it was a good size, and in it he crossed the river. Then he made it small again and put it in his pouch. On and on he walked until he could see the house, and before it the chestnut tree. Then he called a mole out of the ground. The mole came and sniffed around a little plant, the seed of which the heron dearly likes. It is like a bean. Some of these seeds the young lad took and then followed the mole to its hole, and crept under the leaves until he neared the heron. Then he threw the seeds to the bird. The heron saw them and began eating them. Whilst he was occupied and noticed nothing else, the boy filled his bag with chestnuts and set off homewards; but now the heron, no longer occupied with his oh ôñ hi, suspected danger and gave his warning Thr-hr-hr. But the lad was already far away near the great river. Once more he took out his canoe, and was on the water when the women rushed out. They threw a long fish line and caught his canoe to pull him in, but he cut it and got loose. Again the second threw a line and caught him, but again he cut loose, and so on till they had no lines left. So he reached home at length, fearful lest he should find that his brother had died during his absence, but he found him still barely alive, and shouted, "Now, brother, I'm home with the chestnuts, will you have your pipe?" And he began cooking just as his brother liked them, and he narrated all his exploits, and the brother said, "You have done me a great favor, now I shall be well, and we will be happy."

THE GUILTY HUNTERS.

There was a certain tribe whose main occupation was to hunt and to fish. In one of its hunting excursions two families of different clans of this tribe happened to pitch their respective camps quite near to each other. One of these families, in which there was an infant, had very fine luck and the other poor luck. While the father of the child was out hunting, the mother went to a neighboring stream to get some water, but before she dipped her vessel she looked into the water and saw, peering up through the sparkling stream, a very handsome young man with painted cheeks. When her husband returned she told him what she had seen, and, after a consultation, they came to the conclusion that something strange was about to happen, for what the woman had seen was but the reflection of some one hidden in the branches overhanging the stream. They rightly judged that this was an evil omen, and naturally knew that something must be done to avert the impending misfortune, for the woman said that she recognized the face as that of a man from the adjoining camp.

When night came the husband said to his wife, "You and the child must be saved. Go; I shall meet misfortune alone." She then started with the child through the forest, and went on until she came to a hollow log, into which she crept, and then she heard a great noise in the camp, and a voice saying, "You have bitten me." Soon she saw the light of torches borne by people searching for her and the child; nearer and nearer they came, until they reached the log (her hiding-place), into which they pushed their sticks, but the woman remained quiet, and heard them say, "She must be somewhere near here; any way, she cannot live long." She waited until they had left and all was quiet before she emerged from her refuge, and then traveled on as fast as she could until morning, when she came upon a trail, to which, instead of following it, she took a parallel course, and did not see any signs of life until she came to an opening, which appeared like a camping-ground. In the center of this clearing stood a large hemlock tree, into which she climbed, and made herself and child as comfortable as she could.

Soon after ascending the tree she heard approaching voices, one of which said, "We might as well stay here as to go further." They were hunters, heavily laden with skins, meat, &c. During the night one of them said, "My thumb is painful; what shall I say bit me?" The woman heard the answer: "Say a beaver bit you."

In the early dawn the men departed and the woman began to make her way down the tree, but she saw one of the party returning, so she remained until he, finding his bow, again started homeward. When all were out of sight she brought her child down, and, taking again the course parallel to the trail, she hurried onward during the day and reached home just at twilight. When once home she related what had happened to herself, child, and husband, to her many friends who secreted her, and made preparations to have the matter investigated. The head chief was informed, and he sent out "runners" to all the members of the tribe to call them to a general council.

When the time for all to assemble had come, none but the hunters were absent, and they came after repeated and persistent requests to be present. When they did come the head chief said, "We have come to congratulate you in that you have prospered and been preserved from harm. Now, relate to us all the things that have happened to you and tell why you have returned without the other party." The hunters refused to tell anything about their affairs and pretended to know nothing about the other party.

The head chief, after severely cross-examining them, ordered that the woman be brought forth to tell her story. When she had finished her narrative of facts, as stated above, she told that one of them had his thumb bitten, explaining that he was bitten by her husband in defending himself against these robbers, who took from her murdered husband the skins and the meats which they had brought home. Hereupon the head chief gravely said to the waiting and impatient warriors, "Go, do your duty;" and they, with their war-clubs and tomahawks, soon put to death the wicked hunters.

MRS. LOGAN'S STORY.

An old man and his little nephew once lived in a dark woods. One day the man went hunting, and just before leaving told the boy he must not go eastward. But the boy became tired of playing in one place, and was one day tempted to go in the forbidden direction until he came to a large lake, where he stopped to play. While thus engaged a man came up to him and said, "Well, boy, where do you come from?" The boy told him that he came from the woods. Then the man

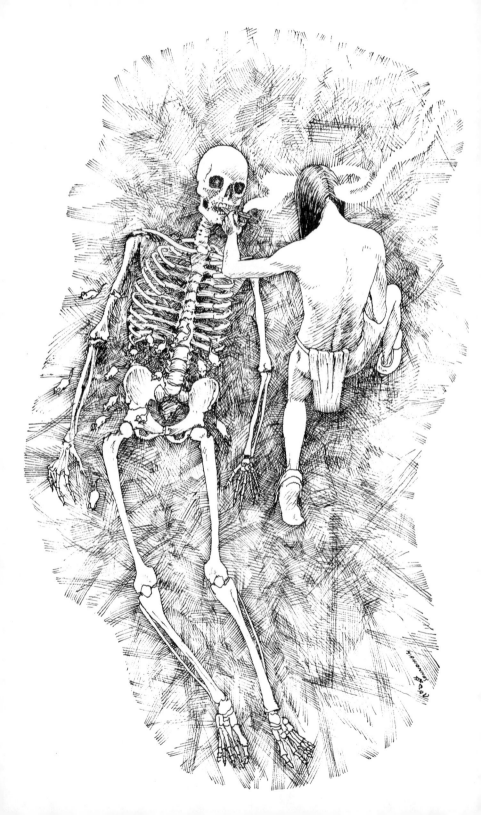

said, "Let us play together at shooting arrows." So they shot off their arrows up into the air, and the boy's arrow went much the higher. Then the man said, "Let us see which can swim the farthest without breathing," and again the boy beat the man. Then the latter said, "Let us go to the island, where you will see many pretty birds." So they entered the canoe. Now, on either side of the canoe were three swans which propelled it. As soon as they were seated in the canoe the man began singing, and very soon they arrived at the island, around which they traveled for some time, and then the man took off all the boy's clothes, and, jumping into his canoe, said, "Come, swans, let us go home," and he began to sing. When the boy perceived that he was deserted he went up the bank and sat down and cried, for he was naked and cold.

It began to grow dark very fast, and he was greatly frightened when he heard a voice say, "Hist! keep still," and, looking around, he saw a skeleton on the ground near him, which beckoned him and said, "Poor boy, it was the same thing with me, but I will help you if you will do something for me." The boy readily consented. Then the skeleton told him to go to a tree near by, and dig on the west side of it, and he would find a tobacco-pouch full of tobacco, a pipe, and a flint; and the boy found them and brought them to the skeleton. It then said, "Fill the pipe and light it;" and he did so. "Put it in my mouth," said the skeleton; and he did so. Then, as the skeleton smoked, the boy saw that its body was full of mice, which went away because of the smoke. Then the skeleton felt better, and told the boy that a man with three dogs was coming to the island that night to kill him, and in order to escape he must run all over the island and jump into the water and out again many times, so that the man would lose the trail. Then, after tracking the island all over, he must get into a hollow tree near by, and stay all night. So the boy tracked the island all over and jumped into the water many times, and at last went into the tree. In the early morning he heard a canoe come ashore, and, looking out, saw another man with three dogs, to whom the man said, "My dogs, you must catch this animal." Then they ran all over the island, but not finding him, the man became so angry that he killed one of the dogs and ate him all up. Then, taking the two remaining, he went away. The boy then came out from his hiding-place, and went to the skeleton, who said, "Are you still alive?" The boy replied, "Yes." "Well," said the skeleton, "the man who brought you here will come to-night to drink your blood, and you must go down to the shore where he will come in, and dig a long pit and lie down in it and cover yourself up with the sand so he cannot see you, and when he comes ashore and is off, you must get into the canoe and say, 'Come, swans, let's go home,' and if the man calls for you to come back you must not turn around or look at him."

The boy promised to obey and soon the man who had brought him came ashore on the island. Then the boy jumped into the canoe, saying,

"Come, swans, let's go to our place;" and as they went he sang just as the man had done. They had gone but a little way when the man saw them. He began to cry, "Come back! Oh, do come back!" but the boy did not look around and they kept on their way. By and by they came to a large rock in which there was a hole, and the swans went up into the rock until they came to a door which the boy proceeded to open. Upon entering the cave he found his own clothes and many others, and also a fire and food all prepared, but no living person. After putting on his clothes he went to sleep for the night. In the morning he found a fire and food, but saw no one.

Upon leaving the cave he found the swans still waiting at the entrance, and, jumping into the canoe, he said, "Come, swans, let's go to the island." When he arrived there he found the man had been killed and nearly eaten up. He then went to the skeleton, which said, "You are a very smart boy; now you must go and get your sister whom this man carried off many years ago. You must start to-night and go east, and by and by you will come to some very high rocks where she goes for water, and you will find her there and she will tell you what to do."

The boy started and in three days arrived at the rocks, where he found his sister, to whom he called, "Sister, come, go home with me"; but she replied, "No, dear brother, I cannot go; a bad man keeps me here, and you must go, for he will kill you if he finds you here." But as the boy would not be persuaded to leave without her she allowed him to stay. Now this very bad man had gone to a great swamp where women and children were picking cranberries. The sister then went to the house and, taking up the planks over which her bed was made, she dug a pit underneath it sufficiently large for her brother to sit in; then she went to her brother and bade him follow her, and to be sure and step in her tracks and not touch anything with his hands or his clothes. So she covered him up in the pit she had prepared for him, and made her bed up again over the place. She then cooked a little boy for the man, put it with wood and water by his bed, and then went and lay down. Soon the man and dogs returned; then immediately the dogs began barking and tearing around as if they were mad. The man said, "You surely have visitors"; she replied, "None but you." And he said, "I know better"; and he took a stick and commanded her to tell him the truth, but she denied it, saying, "Kill me if you like, but I have none." He then went to his bed and sat down to eat his supper; but he said to himself, "She has some one hidden; I will kill him in the morning." He then called her to build a fire, but she replied, "You have wood, build your own fire." Then he said, "Come, take off my moccasins"; but she replied, "I am tired, take them off yourself." Then he said to himself, "Now I know she has seen some one, for she was never so saucy."

In the morning he started off for the swamp to get some children for his dinner. A short distance from home he concealed himself to watch the girl. As soon as he was gone she called her brother and said,

"Come, let us take his canoe and go quickly." So they ran and jumped into the canoe and went off, but the man saw them and ran, throwing a hook which caught the canoe, but as he was pulling it ashore the boy took a stone from the bottom of the canoe and broke the hook. Then they proceeded again very fast. Then the enraged man resorted to another expedient: Laying himself down upon the shore he began to drink the water from the lake, which caused the boat to return very fast. The man continued to drink, until he grew very big with so much water in him. The boy took another stone and threw it and hit the man so it killed him, and the water ran back into the lake. When they saw that he was dead they went back, and the boy said to the two dogs, "You bad dogs, no one will have you now; You must go into the woods and be wolves"; and they started for the woods and became wolves.

Then the boy and his sister went to the island. The boy went to the skeleton, which said, "You are a very smart boy to have recovered your sister—bring her to me." This the boy did, and the skeleton continued, "Now, gather up all the bones you see and put them in a pile; then push the largest tree you see and say, 'All dead folks arise'; and they will all arise." The boy did so, and all the dead arose, some having but one arm, some with but one leg, but all had their bows and arrows.

The boy then said to his sister, "Come, let's go home." When they arrived home they found their own uncle; he looked very old. For ten years he had cried and put ashes upon his head for his little nephew, but now he was very happy to think he had returned.

The boy then told the old man all that he had done, who said, "Let us build a long house." And they did so, and put in six fire-places. Then the boy went back to the island for his people and brought them to the house, where they lived peacefully many years.

THE HUNTER AND HIS DEAD WIFE.

Once upon a time there was a man and his wife who lived in the forest, very far from the rest of the tribe. They used to go hunting together very often, but after a time there were so many things for the wife to do that she staid at home and he went alone. When he went alone he never had good luck. One day the woman was taken sick, and in a day or two she died. The man felt very badly and buried her in the cabin. He was very lonesome; and after a day or two he made a wooden doll about her size and dressed it in the clothes she used to wear. Then he put it down in front of the fire-place and felt better. Then he went hunting; and when he came back he would go up to the doll and brush the ashes off from the face, for as the wood fell down the ashes would rattle onto the face. He had to do his cooking, mending, and making fire, for now there was no one to help him; and so a year passed away. One day when he came home from hunting there was a fire and wood by the door. The next night there was wood and fire and a piece of meat all cooked in the kettle. He looked all over to see who had done this, but could find no one. The next time he went hunting he did not go far and went back quite early, and when he came in sight of the cabin he saw a woman going into the house with wood on her shoulders; he saw, and opened the door quickly, and there was his wife sitting in a chair and the wooden doll was gone. Then she spoke to him, saying, "The Great Spirit felt sorry for you, so he let me come back to see you, but you must not touch me till we have seen all of our people; if you do, you will kill me." So they lived along for some time, when one day the man said, "It is now two years since you died. Let us go home. So you will be well." So he prepared meat for the journey—a string of deer meat for her to carry and one for himself; and so they started. It was going to take them six days to get to the rest of their tribe; when they were within a day's journey of the camp it began to snow, and as they were very weary they lighted fire and partook of food and spread their skins to sleep; but the desire of the man to once more clasp his wife in his arms was too great, and he went up to her and put out his hands; but she motioned him away and said, "We have seen no one yet." He would not listen to her, and he caught her in his arms, and, behold, he was holding the wooden doll! His sorrow was very great. He pushed on to the camp and there he told them all that had befallen him. Some doubted, and they went back with him and found the doll; they also saw the track of the two people in the snow, and the track just like the foot of the doll. The man was ever after very unhappy.

A SURE REVENGE.

Far in the ages of the past, a tribe of the Senecas settled upon the banks of Lake Erie. One eventful winter their enemies, the Illinois, came in great numbers upon the peaceful settlement, surprised the people in their homes, and, in spite of a stout resistance, killed a large number of them and took a middle-aged woman and a boy captive. They started off with the prisoners, and the first day's journey was one of pain and restlessness to the captives. They were foot-sore and weary when camp was pitched for the night. Then around a roaring fire the warriors gloated over the bloody deed. They called the boy and bid him join them in their songs of triumph, adding that they had no desire to hurt him; if he sang well he might enjoy himself. The lad pretended that he could not sing their language, but said that he would sing their song in his tongue, knowing that they could not comprehend a word of it. To this they agreed, and while they shouted out their jubilant delight he repeated, again and again, "I shall never forget what you have done to my people.

You have stolen a helpless woman and a little boy from among them. I shall never forget it. If I am spared you will all lose your scalps." The Illinois warriors understood not a word; they thought he was joining in their triumph, and were satisfied that he would soon forget his own people.

After they had marched three days the woman became exhausted, and she was too faint to be dragged further. The warriors held a council, and she meanwhile spoke to the Seneca boy in earnest tones. "Avenge my blood!" said she; "and when you return to your own people tell them how the cruel Illinois took my life. Promise me you will never cease to be a Seneca." As he finished promising all she asked, she was slain and left dead on the ground.

Then they hurried forward, nearing their own settlement early in the evening. Next day two runners were sent to the village to proclaim their success and return, and all the population turned out with shouts and cries of joy to meet them.

Now the fate of the boy had to be determined. He listened as the chief, with exaggerated gestures and exclamations, gave an account of the successful expedition. The people, as they listened, grew so excited that they beat the ground with their clubs and wished they could exterminate every Seneca in the world. They longed to kill the boy, but the chiefs held a council and decided that there was stuff in him, and they would therefore torture him, and if he stood the test, adopt him into their own tribe. The boy meantime had dreamed a dream, in which he had been forewarned that the Illinois would inflict horrible tortures upon him. "If he can live through our tortures," said the chief, "he shall become an Illinois." The council fire glowed red with burning heat. They seized the captive and held him barefooted on the coals until his feet were one mass of blisters. Then they pierced the blisters with a needle made of fish bone and filled up the blisters with sharp flint stones. "Now run a race," they recommended; "run twenty rods." In his dream he had been told that if he could reach the Long House and find a seat on the wild-cat skin, they would vote him worthy of his life. His agony was intense, but up in his heart rose the memory of his tribe; and as the signal for his start was given he commenced singing with all his might, saying, as they thought, their war song, but in reality the words: "I shall never forget this; never forgive your cruelty. If I am spared you shall every one of you lose your scalps." This gave him courage. He forgot his agony. He bounded forward and flew so swiftly that the Indians, who stood in rows ready to hit him as he passed with thorn-brier branches, could not touch him. He rushed into the Long House; it was crowded, but he spied a wild-cat skin on which an old warrior sat, and he managed to seat himself upon the tail, remembering his dream. The chiefs noticed his endurance and said again, "If we spare his life he will be worthy to become an Illinois; but he knows the trail, so we had better kill him."

A solemn council was held. All the warriors agreed that he had borne the tortures well, and had stuff in him to make a warrior. "He may forget," they said. Still others disagreed and gave their opinion that he ought to be tried still more severely. The majority finally decided that he must die, and in three days should be burned at the stake.

When the day arrived a large fire of pine knots was prepared, and they bound the lad to a stake, and placed him in the midst. Torches were ready to set fire to them, when an old warrior suddenly approached from the forest. It was the chief who had trained other captive Indians. He stood and looked at the boy. Then he said, "His eye is bright. I will take him. I will make a warrior of him. I will inflict our last torture upon him, and if he survives I will adopt him into the tribe." He cut the thongs that bound the boy, and led him away to a spring. "Drink!" he said. And as the lad stooped, he pressed him down under the water until he was well nigh strangled. Three times he subjected him to this barbarity; then as he was still alive, although very weak, he took him to his wigwam and dressed his feet, and told him henceforth he should be an Illinois. No one guessed that revenge was in his heart.

Time passed. He became a man. He had a chief's daughter as his wife. The tribe thought he had lost all memory of his capture. He followed the customs of the Illinois, and was as one of them. He was named Ga-geh-djo-wă. They did not permit him to join them in their warlike expeditions, but he joined in their war dances when they returned. And so as the years passed on he was much esteemed for his feats as a hunter, and his strength and endurance were by-words among the Illinois.

He had been fifteen years among them when he heard them speak of an expedition against the Senecas. He begged to join, and they listened with delight when he declared that he, Ga-geh-djo-wă, would bring home more scalps than any. "He is one of us," they said, and gave him the permission he craved.

Early in the morning the warriors started, and, delighted with his eloquence and readiness to go against his own tribe, they elected him chief of the expedition. They marched on and on for many days, little guessing how his heart beat as they approached the wigwams of the Seneca settlement. He began to issue orders for the attack. "Send scouts," he said, "to the sugar camp, and let them hide in a bush, and return and tell us what they have seen."

Two warriors obeyed his directions, but returned saying there were no signs of the tribe. Then he sent others in a different direction. Their report was the same. Ashes everywhere, they reported, but no smoke and no fires. The Senecas must have left. Then at the council held that night Ga-geh-djo-wă proposed to go himself, with another warrior. This was agreed to, and they set out together. When they had gone five or six miles, the wily chief said to his companion, "Let us separate and each take a different pathway. You go over the hills; I

will go through the valley. We will meet on the mountain at dusk."
So they parted, and Ga-geh-djo-wă, remembering his way, sped where he
guessed he should find some of his old tribe. He found, as he expected,
a family he knew. In hurried words he explained to them their danger:
"The treacherous Illinois are upon you. Warn all the tribe of Senecas:
bid them come early and hide along the range above the valley. I will
be there with a heron's plume on my crest, and when I stumble it is the
signal for the Senecas to attack. Go and tell the word of Ga-geh-djo-wă.
He is true."

Returning to the appointed spot he reported that he had seen nothing,
and hastened back to the camp. Then he said: "I remember these
hills. I know where the Senecas hide. Give me the bravest warriors
and we will go ahead. I can track them to their hiding-place. See!
there below rises the smoke of their wigwams. Send two warriors after
us at a short distance. We will surprise the Senecas."

Early morning saw the camp in activity, every warrior panting for
the scalps he yearned to procure. Little they dreamed that already five
hundred Senecas awaited them in the valley. The march commenced.
As they entered the valley Ga-geh-djo-wă gazed anxiously around and
delightedly caught sight of a face among the bushes. Now he knew
the Senecas had heeded him. He led his men forward; then, pretending to miss his footing, he fell. Instantly the war-cry sounded; the
Senecas rushed from their ambush, and he left his treacherous foes and
rejoined his own people.

The slaughter was great. All the Illinois warriors but two in the rear
were slain. Three hundred scalps revenged the treachery of the Illinois. Ga-geh-djo-wă was seized by the jubilant Senecas and borne in
triumph to their settlement. Around the fires, as they displayed the
scalps of their enemies, they listened to his recital of their cruelty, of
his tortures, and of the woman's death. Never again did he leave them.
He lived many years, the most esteemed warrior and chief of the Senecas, and when he died they buried him with the highest honors they
knew, and have kept his name sacred in the legends of the tribe to this
day.

TRAVELER'S JOKES.

An Indian traveler, tired of his uneventful journey, undertook to cre-
ate an excitement after the following fashion: An old Indian custom
is for runners, or those carrying important news, to announce the fact
and gather the people together by crying, in singing tones, "Goh-weh,
goh-weh." This the traveler began doing, and when the crowd called
upon him to stop and tell his news, he began, "As I came through the
last village the people were so delighted with my news that they all
danced for joy, and shouted and kissed me." This he told so earnestly

and sincerely that the people, not wishing to be outdone by any other tribe, also began singing and kissing him and making merry ; and while the excitement was at its height, pleased with his success, the facetious traveler escaped and continued his journeyings.

Arrived at the next village he again began calling, "Goh-weh, goh-weh"; and the people and chiefs gathered around him, crying, "Let us hear." And he answered, "As I passed through the last town some people wept at my news, others began quarreling, kicking, and fighting." Immediately his contagious news produced its effect, and in the confusion he again escaped, saying to himself " What fools people are."

That night, as he was preparing to camp out, a man passed who inquired the distance to the next village; but the traveler said, " You cannot reach it to-night. Let us camp together." As they were each recounting stories, and the new-comer was boasting of his superior cunning, the traveler inquired, " What log is that you now use for a pillow ?" and he guessed hickory, elm, &c. But the traveler said, "No, it is everlasting sleep." In the morning the traveler took some pitchy resin and rubbed over the eyes of his sleeping comrade and left, laughing at the probable chagrin the man would feel when attempting to open his eyes, and in the recollection of the warning regarding everlasting sleep and his boasts of superior cunning.

No further accounts of the traveler's jokes are told.

KINGFISHER AND HIS NEPHEW.

An old man and his nephew were living together in a good home near the river, where they enjoyed themselves day after day. One morning the old man said to his nephew, "When you are a man, remember in hunting never to go west; always go to the east."

The young man reflected and said to himself, " Why should this be so?" My uncle To-bé-se-ne always goes west, and brings home plenty of fish. Why should he tell me not to go? Why does he never take me with him ?"

He made up his mind at last that he would go, never minding about the advice. So he set off in a roundabout way, and as he passed the marsh land near the river he saw his uncle. "Ha!" he thought, "now I know where he catches his fish"; and he watched him take from his pocket two sharp sticks and put them in his nose, and then plunge into deep water and come up with a nice fish. He watched him carefully and then returned home. Presently the uncle came back, bringing some nice fish, but he never guessed that the nephew had seen him.

The young man now felt certain that he could fish as well as his uncle. Accordingly, one day when the old man had gone deer hunting, he thought it a good opportunity to try the new method. He hunted

among his uncle's things until he found two sticks, and then he set off
to the same log where he had seen his uncle sitting, which projected
above the water in the river.   He saw the fishes swimming about, so he
at once stuck the two sticks into his nose, and plunged in.   Then the
sticks went deep into his nose and made it ache dreadfully, and he felt
very sick.   Home he hurried and lay down, thinking he should die of
the agony.   When his uncle came home he heard him groaning, and
said, "What ails you?   Are you sick?"   "Yes, uncle," replied he, "I
think I shall die.   My head is sore and pains me."   "What have you been
about?" asked the uncle, severely.   "I have been fishing," confessed the
young man; "I took your things, and I know I have done wrong."   "You
have done very wrong," said the uncle; but he took the pincers and drew
out the sticks, and the young man promised never again to fish in the
west, and got well.

After a while, however, he thought that he would go and see once
more, although he had been forbidden.   So he started west.   He heard
boys laughing, and he had none to play with, so he joined them.   They
invited him to swim with them and he accepted, and they had a very
gay time together.   At last they said, "It is time to go home; you go,
too."   Then he saw that they had wings, and they gave him a pair and
said, "There is an island where all is lovely; you have never been up
there—over the tall tree up in the air; come."   So they started up in
the air, far away above the trees, till they could see both sides of the
river; and he felt very happy.   "Now," said they, "you can see the
island"; and he looked down and saw the print of their tracks on the
island; so he knew they had been there.   Then said they, "Let us go in
swimming again."   So they went into the water.   Then they said, "Let
us see which can go down and come up the farthest"; and they tried
one at a time, and he was the last, so he must go the farthest; and while
he was in the water the rest put on their wings and, taking his also,
flew up in the air.   He plead in vain for them to wait; but they called,
as though speaking to some one else, "Uncle, here is game for you
to-night."   Then they flew away in spite of his entreaties, and he thought
to himself, "I shall surely be destroyed, perhaps by some animal."

As he looked around he perceived tracks of dogs which had clawed
the different trees, and then he concluded that perhaps they would tear
him to pieces.   In order to confuse them in their scent he climbed each
tree a little way, and so went on until he reached the last tree on the
island, in which he remained and listened in suspense.   He soon heard
a canoe on the river and some one calling the dogs.   Then he concluded
his conjectures were true.   After making a fire the man sent out his
dogs.   The man had a horrid-looking face, both behind and before,
which the poor nephew could see by the fire-light.   Then the dogs began barking, having traced the tracks to the first tree; they made such
a noise that the man concluded they had found the game, and went to
the tree, but found nothing.   So they went on to the next, and the next,

with the same experience, and this they continued the night long. Then the old man said, very angrily, "There is no game here; my nephews have deceived me." And he returned, leaving the last tree.

After sunrise the poor fellow came down from the tree, saying, "I think I have escaped, for if those young fellows return I will watch them and contrive to get their wings from them." He then concealed himself and patiently awaited their coming. He soon heard their voices, saying, "Now we will have a good time." They first jumped around to warm themselves, and then said, "Let us all dive together." Then he rushed out, and, taking all the wings, he put on one pair, and flew away, calling out, "Uncle, now there is plenty of game for you"; and when they entreated him he replied, "You had no mercy on me; I only treat you the same." Then he flew on until he came to his old home, where he found his old uncle, to whom he recounted the whole story; and after that time he remained peacefully at home with his good uncle, where he still resides.

"So many times my old grandfather, chief Warrior, told me that story," said Zachariah Jamieson to me on the Seneca Reservation.

THE WILD-CAT AND THE WHITE RABBIT.

[Told by Zachariah Jamieson.]

The wild cat, roaming disconsolately in the woods, experienced the sense of utter loneliness which calls for companionship. A friend he must have or die. Cats there were none within speaking distance, but rabbits it might be possible to entice. He commenced a plaintive ditty. His soul craved a white rabbit above all else, and his song was pathetic enough to entice the most obdurate :

> He gah yah neh
> He gah yah! He găh yăh
> Di ho ni shu guă da-se
> He yah gah.

His meaning was simple as his song, "When you are frightened, sweet rabbit, you run in a circle."

He was wise in his generation. A short distance off lay a white rabbit in his lair; hearing the melodious ditty he pricked up his ears. "Heigho!" exclaimed he, "that dangerous fellow, the wild-cat, is around; I hear his voice; I must scud"; and away he ran, turning from the direction in which the voice came and hastening with all his might. He had gone but a short distance when he stopped, turned back his ears and listened. There was the song again :

> He găh yăh! He găh yăh!
> Di ho—

He waited to hear no more. On he sped for a while ; then once more he laid back his ears and halted again; surely this time the song was nearer. He was still more frightened. " I will go straight on" said he; but he thought he was following an opposite direction. On and on he sped, scarce daring to breathe; then a pause; alas! the singer is nearer—nearer yet. Unfortunate rabbit! he could but follow his instinct and run in a circle which brought him each time nearer his enemy. Still the song went on, until, circling ever nearer, white rabbit fell a victim to the wild-cat.

CHAPTER VI.

RELIGION.

In a former chapter it was concluded that the "Great Spirit" is the Indian's conception of the white man's God. This belief in God is common now to all of the Iroquois, but the Christian religion is professed by only about one-half of their number. The other half of the people are usually denominated "pagans." The so-called Christian Indians are distributed among various sects, worship in churches, and profess Christian creeds.

The pagan Indians worship the sun, moon, stars, thunder, and other spirits rather vaguely defined. But though in talking with white men they frequently speak of the Great Spirit, yet in their worship there seems to be no very well-defined recognition of the same, the term being used in a confused manner. Their religious rites are chiefly in the form of festivals.

Among these so-called pagan Iroquois of to-day no private worship is known, unless the offering of burning tobacco to Hinu^n, or the occasional solitary dance, as practiced by some of the squaws, be so considered.

The annual public national and religious festivals are eight in number, with the occasional addition of those specially appointed. As the nucleus to the ceremonies observed at these festivals we find many of their ancient practices retained, such as dancing, games, the use of incense, &c. And upon these have been grafted, according to their peculiar interpretation, varied forms from the Romish, Jewish, or Protestant churches, which to them seemed suitable and adaptable. Although the Tuscaroras of western New York retain many of the old superstitions none of the national festivals are there observed, and hardly a trace now remains of their old religious customs.

About half of the Senecas still adhere to paganism, but it is only among the Onondagas that all the old festivals are strictly and religiously observed, after the sequence and manner of the following account of the New-Year Festival:

NEW-YEAR FESTIVAL.

At the first new moon of the new year, which sometimes occurs three weeks after New Year's Day, the chiefs assemble and call what they term a "holy meeting," the order of which is as follows: A bench or table is placed in the center of the circle of chiefs, upon which are placed their strings of Indian wampum. One then rises and makes a long speech, in which he introduces the sayings, maxims, and teachings o Handsome Lake, who, nearly a century ago, introduced a new form into the Seneca religion. Speeches of this kind occupy four days. On the fifth day the principal chiefs, taking hold of the wampum, say: "I put all my words in this wampum"; "I have been drunk"; or, "I have sinned," &c. On the sixth day the warriors go through the same form of confession. On the following day the chiefs pass the wampum around among the assembly.

At the conclusion of this portion of their ceremonies the U-stu-ä-gu-nä, or feather dance, sometimes called the dance of peace, is performed. For this there is a particular costume, by which it must always be accompanied. The dance is simple. Two men are chosen to stand in the center and are encircled by dancers.

After this dance the clans are divided for the games as follows:

Bear			Wolf.
Deer			Beaver.
Eel	against		Snipe.
Hawk			Turtle.

The clans thus divided hold their feasts in separate houses, even although husband and wife be divided. On the fourth day each of these divisions, singing a chant, repairs to the Council House. The gambling then commences and continues three more days. The gambling and betting concluded, two Indians, costumed as medicine men, run into all the houses, and raking up the ashes call on all to repair to the Council House. In the evening of this day begins the "scaring of witches"; speeches are made; Indian songs or chants are sung the while an old man or woman enters, appearing to wish or search for something, the assembly guessing at the object desired. Should the guess be correct, a reply of "thank you" is made. He or she receives it, and as a return proceeds to dance.

On the following evening a number of Indians in frightful costumes enter on their knees, yelling and groaning. Shaking their rattles, they proceed to the council fire, where they stir up the ashes. The chiefs then present to them Indian tobacco, and they are commanded to perform all the errands and act as the messengers for the evening.

On this same evening it is given forth that on the ensuing day, at a given hour, the white dog will be roasted. For this purpose a perfectly pure, unblemished white dog is selected, and five young men of the most spotless reputation are chosen to kill the dog, around whose neck two ropes are fastened, and the young men then pull the ropes till the dog is strangled. When dead it is presented to the victorious gambling party, who proceed to comb out its hair carefully with teasels. It is then decorated with wampum, ribbons, Indian tobacco, strips of buckskin, small baskets, silver brooches, &c.

The four winning clans then form in a circle around the dog and the four leading chiefs. The first chief chants around the dog; the second puts it upon his back ; the third carries an extra basket trimmed with beads, brooches, and ribbons, and filled with Indian tobacco; the fourth chief, bareheaded and scantily clothed, follows as they pass in Indian file to the other Council House, where the defeated division makes an offering, which is accepted by the fourth chief. All then proceed to gether to the appointed place for the dog roasting. While the fire is being lighted the chiefs chant and praise the Great Spirit, after which, while the warriors are shooting up at the sun, the dog is thrown into the fire, which ceremony unites all the clans. This is followed by chants. The leading chief then gives notice of the dance for the following day. At this first day of rejoicing or dancing the "feather dance" is repeated, and a chant is sung which embraces almost the entire language of the Protestant Episcopal canticle, *Benedicite omnia opera Domini ;* but the translation, in place of commanding the works of God to render him praise, praises the works themselves. Instead of " O ye angels of the Lord," that passage is rendered, "O ye four persons who made us and have charge of us, we praise thee," &c.

The feast then follows, consisting of meats garnished with sunflower oil, &c. The third day of dancing is devoted to the war dance, which is dedicated to the sun, moon, stars, and thunder. The feather dance is again introduced, the women this time participating in it. In itself the dance is very monotonous, except for the variety introduced by whooping, beating the floor with the war clubs, occasional speeches, and offerings to the dancers.

At the conclusion of the feather dance the Si-ti-gă-ni-ai, or shuffle dance, follows. This is executed solely by the women, who do not lift their feet from the floor. The men keep time by drumming and using the rattles. Then succeeds the guide dance, performed as follows: Two or four men stand inside a circle and sing a dance song, while all the people join in the dance in pairs, the couples facing each other. Consequently, two out of each four have to go backwards, but at a signal in the music all change places. This is invariably the closing dance of the new year's festival, but it is then arranged that seven days later the medicine men shall all reappear, and for a day and a night go about in the houses and chase away all diseases, &c. This closes by all repairing to the Council House, where a large kettle of burnt corn, sweetened with maple sugar, is prepared for the medicine men, who eat it from the kettle. From this Council House fire the medicine men throw the ashes upon the assembled people for the purpose of dispelling witches and disease. This concludes the new year's festival ceremonies after a duration of three weeks.

TAPPING THE MAPLE TREES.

The next public service is at the tapping of the maple trees, and consists of the war dance, the performance of which will, it is hoped, bring on warmer weather and cause the sap to flow.

As a special favor to ambitious parents, the dancing warriors often bear in their arms infant boys, who are supposed to become early inured and inspired with a desire for a warrior life.

At the close of the sugar season follows the maple-sugar festival, the soups of which are all seasoned with the newly-made sugar. This festival, in which a number of dances are introduced, lasts but one day.

PLANTING CORN.

The corn-planting festival is very similar to that of the new year, introducing the confession of sins by the chiefs, the feather dance, &c. This lasts seven days.

STRAWBERRY FESTIVAL.

During the strawberry season, at a time appointed previously by the chiefs, the women proceed to the fields and gather the berries. The great feather dance follows; afterwards two children carry about a vessel containing the berries, mixed with water and sugar, and present it to each person, who is expected to give thanks as he receives it. More dancing ensues.

The bean festival next occurs and is very similar to the strawberry festival.

GREEN-CORN FESTIVAL.

This is preceded by a hunt by the warriors for deer or bear meat to use for the soups.

During their absence the ceremony of confession takes place, as in the New Year's festival, and the women are engaged in roasting the corn preparatory to its being placed in the kettle with the beans for the succotash. If the weather is very warm the hunters bring home the meat ready baked. On their return the feasting and dancing commence and continue for four days. The gambling, which is considered a religious ceremony, is then introduced, silver brooches, war clubs, jewelry, bead work, &c., being used as the wagers. Sometimes the clans play against each other, but frequently the women play against the men, and are oftener the winning party.

This festival is the gala season of the Indian year, and all appear in their most fanciful decorations, some of the costumes having an intrinsic value of several hundred dollars.

GATHERING THE CORN.

The last public festival of the year is at the gathering of the corn. After the thanksgiving dance there is a repetition of the confession of sins and the feather dance. In the latter the gayly-colored corn is used as a decoration, sometimes whole strings of it, still upon the cob, being worn as ornaments.

The above form the eight public yearly festivals of the Iroquois, but occasionally other dances are introduced. Among these are the raccoon dance and the snake dance, the latter being similar to the guide dance, but partaking more of a gliding, snake-like motion.

Private dances are held by the medicine men, in which are introduced the Kâ-nai-kwä-ai, or eagle dance; the Tai-wa-nu-ta-ai-ki, or dark dance, performed in the dark; the Ka-hi-tu-wi, or pantomime dance; and the W-na-tai-nu-u-ni, or witches' dance. On the death of a medicine man a special dance is held by his fraternity, and, during the giving of certain medicines, medicine tunes are chanted. No dances are held upon the death of private individuals, but at the expiration of ten days a dead feast is celebrated and the property of the deceased is distributed by gambling or otherwise. Occasionally speeches are made, but no singing or dancing is indulged in, except during a condolence council, when deceased chiefs are mourned and others chosen in their places.

Private dances are not infrequently given by individual members of the tribe, who, having conceived a great affection for each other, publicly cement it by a friendship dance.

Erminnie Adele Smith, 1836 - 1886

Photo courtesy of National Anthropological Archives, Smithsonian
Institution, Washington, D.C., U.S.A. (negative 44,730).
From a group photo, Officers of the American Association for the
Advancement of Science, Ann Arbor, Michigan, 1885.

THE BEAUTY AND HER SNAKE LOVER

Brown North Carolina Steatite (aka: *Tuscarora Stone*) by Hōyanā**˝**tōn̲, Onondaga, Six Nations Reserve, carved in the early 1970's.

There once was a very haughty woman whose pride in her beauty was such that she found no man equal in appearance and would marry no suitor.

It happened that one day a stranger appeared in her village who was exceedingly handsome and well dressed. Here was a man worthy of her, and she married him.

One day her husband lay with his head in her lap while she groomed his hair. Suddenly, to her horror, his body changed into that of a snake. Thus was she rewarded for her vanity... the snake is the most dreaded and loathsome of all creatures to the Iroquois.

This is a variant of a much longer story recorded by Curtin and Hewitt in: *Seneca Fiction, Legends, and Myths*, pages 86-90.   WGS

Photo by C. Koennecke

PUNISHING THE WITCH
Mottled green Québec Steatite by Owēdrōn⁽'gyoⁿ, Cayuga, Six Nations Reserve, carved in the early 1970's.

The Messengers who brought the Creator's revelations to the Iroquois through the medium of Chief Handsome Lake, June 15, 1799, recounted the great evils which they committed that offended Him. The second of the four major sins was the practice of witchcraft. Witches must desist, repent, and live in harmony with others.

Punishment for discovered, or suspected, witches could range from whipping to death. In an incident recounted to the faithful in the *CODE* a woman and her daughter were administered a public flogging at Cold Spring, Allegany Reservation, in the early 1800's; similar incidents are recorded in the literature. A fear of witches obsesses many people to the present.

See: *The Code of Handsome Lake, the Seneca Prophet*, A. C. Parker, pages 27-29; 46.

WGS

A YOUNG MAN SAVED BY *TOAD*   Brown North Carolina Steatite (aka: *Tuscarora Stone*) by Hiʔsas, Cayuga, Six Nations Reserve, carved in the early 1970's.

A youth was fleeing through the forest, pursued by a witch. He encountered a stranger who offered help. When this was accepted the stranger stooped down; he was *TOAD*. The youth got on his back. *TOAD* stretched until his legs were very long, then he hurled the young man to safety on a far-off hill.

See: *Seneca Indian Myths*, J. Curtin, pages 303-306.   WGS

IROQRAFTS Indian Reprint Series

Catalogue Number	Title	ISBN-0-919645-
24-00300	**Scalping and Torture: Warfare Practices Among North American Indians** by Frederici, Nadeau, Knowles	-10-0
24-00301	**Hair Pipes in Plains Indian Adornment** by J. C. Ewers	-11-9
24-00302	**Indians of Ontario** by J. L. Morris	-12-7
24-00303	**Wildwood Wisdom** by E. Jaeger	-14-3
24-00304	**Indian Uses of Wild Plants** by F. Densmore	-16-X